GIVE IT UP!

GIVE IT UP!

MY YEAR OF LEARNING

TO LIVE BETTER

WITH LESS

Mary Carlomagno

WILLIAM MORROW

An Imprint of HarperCollins*Publishers*

HarperCollins books may be purchased for educational, business, or sales promotional use. For information please write: Special Markets Department, HarperCollins Publishers, 10 East 53rd Street, New York, NY 10022.

FIRST EDITION

Designed by Betty Lew

Printed on acid-free paper

Library of Congress Cataloging-in-Publication Data

Carlomagno, Mary.
    Give it up!: my year of learning to live better with less /
Mary Carlomagno.
p.   cm.
ISBN-13: 978-0-06-078980-0
ISBN-10: 0-06-078980-8
1. Simplicity. 2. Self-denial. 3. Carlomagno, Mary. I. Title.

BJ1496.C37 2006
179'.9—dc22   2005050222

06 07 08 09 10 ❖/QW 10 9 8 7 6 5 4 3 2 1

ACKNOWLEDGMENTS

I would like to thank my agent, Marly Rusoff, whose patience and wisdom are a true gift. Thank you to Michael Morrison for giving the book a home. Special thanks to Harriet Bell for her thoughtful work as editor and to Pamela Canon for guiding the process so beautifully.

To my special friends, Pat Eisemann for being my Burgess Meredith, Judy Collins for providing shelter in a storm, Jan Lindstrom for her wit and guidance, Carolyn Mann for her endless encouragement, Lisa Johnson for making the lightbulb appear, and the wildly sophisticated Nicole Williams for starting me on the journey.

Special thanks to my book pals Edward and Sessalee.

Bottomless gratitude to my family and friends for supporting the road less taken, especially my mother for providing a lifetime of inspiration.

GIVE IT UP!

Introduction

We must be the change we wish in the world.
—MAHATMA GANDHI

When I set out to write this book, my intention was to eliminate unnecessary facets of life, in essence to determine what I could live without. Accustomed to the frantic pace of the world around me, I had a nagging feeling that something was missing. Each day was much the same, providing the everyday routines all dependent on the same rituals. Reading the entire newspaper was out of habit, not out of need. Habitually checking voice mail and cell phone was more than just a convenience, it had become obsession. Shopping had reached an all-time high, where multiple versions of the same item were purchased again and again without my realizing that that item already hung in my closet at home in other colors. I was in need of a change.

One morning, while trying to decide which pair of shoes to wear, I was behind schedule and was clearly going to be late for work. To make matters worse, while reaching for my black sling backs, an avalanche of designer shoeboxes hit me squarely on the head. For some people, a subtle signal can lead to a change in life; others need a stronger message. In my case, it was being literally hit over the head with my own shoes. This was my wake-up call.

Later that morning, I plunked down $4.20 for a mocha grande at my local coffee shop. I reached for my cell phone to check voice mail and make a mental note of the meetings planned for that day; I wondered how my life got so complicated, with too many distractions: too much stuff and too much technology demanding attention and taking my focus.

Raised as a Catholic, I was required to observe Lent by sacrificing something that was dear to honor our faith. "What are you giving up for Lent?" my three older brothers would challenge. For forty days, we would give up candy, soda, or dessert. Reading about Lent as an adult, I learned that according to the Church, sacrifices made during Lent should be life changing. In fact, some believe that those who truly experience Lent emerge as a completely new person. Standing in the coffee shop that morning I recalled the experience of Lent and began to wonder if I could give up any of these things that now seemed so essential. Would it be possible to live without a hundred boxes of designer shoes, costly microbrewed coffee, expensive handbags, or the ever-present cell phone that fueled my everyday existence?

Perhaps eliminating these items and habits would create an appreciation for everything that I was already so fortunate to have. Each month for one year, I would choose one of my favorite things and give it up cold turkey. This would be my year of living better with less.

Each monthly choice has a personal and significant "ouch" factor for me, a profound feeling of discomfort that accompanied the mere suggestion of living an entire month without chocolate, elevators, or television. My selections were designed to push me out of my traditional comfort zone, where a change in habits would force uneasiness, questions, and finally scrutiny. My insatiable desire for "stuff" was stimulated by a consumerist society that encourages purchasing faster, newer, and better products.

Consumers like me get instantaneous gratification, however fleeting, through the latest cell phone, iPod, or digital camera. We wear our trendy shoes while ordering a computer that will arrive at our door the next day. We try a new diet plan and strive to lose fifteen pounds in one week without exercise. We drive custom-built SUVs off the lot with no money down. This self-improvement craze has created a frenzy of makeovers to make us better. But what if we were to turn the tables on this trend and make ourselves over from the inside out, not the outside in.

As I challenged myself over the course of the year, each month presented its own surprising and unique revelation. Giving up shopping made for a more creative personal style. Without a cell phone, I learned how to communicate better. Taking the stairs instead of elevators made me more aware of my physical body. The recurring lesson each month distinguished the difference between deprivation and sacrifice. With sacrifice, a conscious decision is made to go without; deprivation sets up a helpless longing, a feeling that I rarely encountered.

This year of living without forced me to put my habits of accumulation on hold, ultimately giving way to an awareness and enjoyment of the things in life that I was blessed to have and be part of: reading poetry, taking a walk or bike ride, or enjoying a great meal with friends. For me, the biggest lesson of all was not about what I had given up, but what I had gained.

January

ALCOHOL

I feel sorry for people who don't drink. When they wake up in the morning that's as good as they're going to feel all day.

—FRANK SINATRA

When I woke up on January 1 with flannel on my teeth, a tribal pounding in my head, and a feeling of mental queasiness that could only be remedied by a Denny's Grand Slam breakfast, I uttered those famous last words, "I am never drinking again," followed by those other famous words, "I mean it."

Even though at that moment I was in no position to make clear decisions, I needed to regain control of my life or at least my ability to stand up without the room spinning. Push had come to shove and I was ready to strike a deal. At that point, I would have done just about anything to feel better.

This roller-coaster ride was the end result of mandatory fun planned by my friends. We attended the mother of all New Year's Eve parties, in one of the largest bars in New York. Judging by the line out the door, it seemed likely that one, if not all, of our soul mates awaited inside. Once through the door, we quickly grabbed a table by the bar, where we made our presence known to both the bartender and our potential soul mates. We simultaneously made our way to the bottom of many glasses and to the bottom of as many pickup lines. Finding our soul mates soon became less and less likely.

Adding insult to injury, the party was not only physically taxing, as evidenced by the worst hangover of my life, but expensive as well. The all-inclusive cost for the night of fun was equivalent to that of a pair of Bergdorf loafers I had been eyeing. Open bar, food, noisemakers, and music were promised along with the implied message that you were going to have the time of your life. The reality was that except for one French-fry plate, all of the above were conspicuously missing, with the exception of my favorite cocktail, the dirty martini. Always a believer in getting my money's worth, or in this case my loafers' worth, I bellied up to the bar again and again.

According to www.familydoctor.org, a woman is considered to be drinking excessively if she has more than seven drinks per week and more than three drinks per occasion. A man is considered to be drinking excessively if he has more than fourteen drinks per week or more than four drinks per occasion. I had surpassed my drinking limit with the New Year's cocktails alone. At last count, the score was Martinis: 7 Mary: 0. Clearly my parameters for a night of casual drinking were completely out of balance with reality. According to the National Institute on Alcohol Abuse and Alcoholism, a drink is generally considered to be 12 ounces of beer, 5 ounces of wine, or 1.5 ounces of 80-proof distilled spirits. Each of these drinks contains roughly the same amount of absolute alcohol—approximately 0.5 ounce, or 12 grams. And while it seemed reasonable to follow the recommendations of the medical profession, I wondered how in the world I was going to stop drinking for an entire month.

Temptations popped up everywhere like Viagra ads on the Internet. Even so, as the month began, I was overly confident. At first, the mere smell of alcohol seemed repugnant to me. This challenge should not be hard for someone like me, I reasoned, who has excellent decision-making abilities and tremendous willpower. After all, it was not for the rest of my life.

My first obstacle presented itself while reviewing my weekly calendar, which had the words "drinks with . . ." written at the bottom of almost every page. Would it be possible for me to have a conversation with a work colleague or with a girlfriend at a bar and order club soda? I started making the phone calls.

There were two choices: Ask if I could reschedule for after February 1, when the drinking would resume and I would be "normal" again, or keep the date and rely on virgin cocktails to keep the conversation going. My first three phone calls resulted in three rescheduled drink dates for February when, according to one of my friends, "I would come to my senses." Another friend suggested, "Let's wait till we can both have fun." So, with three for three on the rescheduling, February began to look like one big drunken month. Even though an occasional friend would applaud my efforts, their disbelief in my ability to pull it off reinforced the "better you than me" adage.

The fourth call to my brother was illuminating. He

is a self-described food and wine snob who once asked me on the way to Sunday Mass what kind of wine would be served. He had managed to get a reservation at New York's Veritas, which has a world-class wine list. I called to tell him that I would still be happy to attend, but that I would not be drinking anything alcoholic, including wine. After a moment of silence, he suggested rescheduling the evening. Neither one of us could see the point of having this amazing meal without wine. Rescheduling this dinner made me realize the many roles alcohol played in my life.

As a marketing professional, I attended cocktail parties, award dinners, and launch parties several times each week where cocktails, wine, and champagne were served from the moment you walked in the room until the event ended. Would I be able to let those drinks trays pass me by and carry on conversation with co-workers and clients?

Even if there wasn't a work-related party, it was easier to meet with colleagues after five "for drinks" than to get them on the phone during the day. It seemed that no one had the time to talk at work anymore. Drinks after work became a necessity for bonding with co-workers and talking to colleagues. We found ourselves spending more and more time in the office, and by the time we were ready to leave, heading to the bar at the end of the day was as important as the first cup of coffee at the beginning. How else could we talk about our co-workers, since they sat right next to us, all day long? The bar was our neutral zone, our Switzerland.

I rescheduled two January drinks dates with people from work without too much explanation. It was much easier for me to say that I had a conflict than tell them the real reason for the postponement. The path of least resistance became my road map.

Once all of the rescheduling was taken care of, I found myself with almost all of my evenings free. I eagerly looked forward to unwinding from the hectic routine of holiday parties, last-minute shopping, and endless eating and drinking. I became a recluse for those two weeks, avoiding any situation where I might be tempted to have a drink. Our advertising agency's Ketel One New Year's toast I turned down, as well as a literary launch party held at an Irish bar. I knew myself well enough to realize that both occasions were impossible for me to attend without giving in to the demon.

After two weeks of restraint and alone time, I was feeling isolated and craved social interaction. I became concerned when I started to memorize the prime-time lineups of all the major networks. Surely, becoming a recluse and avoiding social interaction wasn't the answer. Why couldn't I socialize but not drink? After all of the scheduling and rescheduling, I decided to attack my social calendar with the same vigor I always had, but without alcohol. When meeting my friends for drinks, I would order "just a club soda." Having a drink meant an alcoholic drink, a mojito, a tequila sunrise; club soda did not fill the order. Becoming comfortable with my self-imposed ban on my own was hard enough, but going public was another thing entirely. We have all heard the phrase "you should not drink alone."

My first night out was at Tonic. The waiter came over and took our orders: vanilla vodka and soda, a Heineken, a glass of merlot, and for you, miss? I hesitated, looked around at the people at the table, apologized for stalling, and mumbled, "Just a club soda." The entire table stopped their conversation and looked at me. My friend Sally blurted out, "Why are you drinking club soda, what's wrong with you?" She acted as if I had some sort of malady that made me delusional enough to order a nonalcoholic beverage. I explained the reason for my seemingly bizarre behavior. On the surface, they seemed to understand, at least they all nodded "yes" in unison. Although they were supportive, I knew they harbored a bit of suspicion as the focus of the night was drinks, and soda was just not part of that club. Oddly, a subtle mistrust came into play. They were convinced that I would take record of what took place and report back to some governing body at the food and beverage committee.

Drinking is like a group activity or team sport—if one member is not playing his or her part, it affects the whole game. My abstinence set off the group dynamic and created a palpable tension among us. In the past, I was always the first one to break down reluctant friends and coerce them into having a drink. I would expect the rest of the group to keep pace, which meant at least two drinks per outing. That night, I took notice: Every time the waiter came back to serve another drink to one or more people from the group, the others would order in turn, and an unspoken approval was exchanged. The words "will you have another one?" when accompanied by "we all would like another round" held the group together. Ordering another round implied an unspoken commitment that bonded the drinkers. As if ordering together meant they enjoyed each other's company and did not want to leave, all because of these magic cocktails. I wondered if I could feel the same level of bonding with "just a club soda." Now that I was considered an afterthought to the serious drinker, the waiter and the group skipped me: "Since you are only having a club soda, you must not need another drink."

Now that I was firmly planted on the outside of the libations circle, I was able to observe my behavior as well as that of my drinking buddies. I was becoming that spy they feared. Instead of feeling proud of my willpower, I still needed to think up excuses for my no tippling policy. Acceptable reasons for not drinking were difficult to think of. The only solid ones that I could come up with were "I am on antibiotics" or "I had a rough night last night." The antibiotic line did not prove to be valid, as very few people I know subscribe to this medical advice. Some of them consider it to be an old wives' tale. As for drinking the night before, the jig was up, since everyone knew that I had not been drinking the night before.

Why was I trying to come up with excuses for not drinking? It certainly could not be peer pressure, which I conquered in high school when I was riddled with remorse after taking part in a cruel joke that made a classmate wear pajamas to a pep rally. Yet, that evening in the bar, being bullied by my friends to have a "real drink," made me feel like that pajama-clad classmate. For a few desperate moments, I planned a social escape, which included a choice between exclaiming, "No means no!" at the top of my lungs or explaining the timeless virtue of Nancy Reagan's 1980s abstinence campaign, neither of which made sense, as the next table's cosmopolitans began to mock me. Images of Carrie at the prom went through my mind as I was feeling unlucky, oddly enough, in a bar called Taboo.

I was reminded of freshman year at college where the getting-to-know-you dialogue usually included an inquiry about whether I was someone who "partied" or not. Happy that I was being talked to and eager to fit in, I answered, "Yes, of course, doesn't everyone?" Clad in Z Cavaricci pants and a gravity-defying hairdo, I became a cool partyer. And while my college education is certainly valuable and my college friends are still in my life, the lessons learned during those formative social events at frat parties, in college dorms, and at local pubs shaped my attitudes and opinions about alcohol for years to come. The cool people were drinking. Drinking was fun. Drink and everyone will like you. These basic tenets became gospel.

As I sat in the hip martini lounge years later and

proceeded to order club soda rather than my customary dirty Ketel One, I began to examine my habit of caving in, having a drink automatically, regardless whether I wanted one or not. Thankfully, this time not only was I better dressed, but I had a new clarity that allowed me to finally answer that freshman year question, do you party? This month, my answer was "no." I still felt cool.

With this first awkward social engagement under my belt, I was gaining more confidence in my newfound ability to "just say no" to the cocktail—and, more important, to the peer pressure—but there was something still gnawing at me. This need for cocktails and the social interaction linked to drinking required more examination on my part. Sure, I could tough out another few weeks of club soda and cranberry mixers, but my curiosity ran deeper. Giving up something to prove to yourself that you can was why I began Liquor Lent. Now I wanted to learn more about myself, my relationships, and more important, my reluctance to give up this social drink circuit.

There is nothing quite as sobering as being the only nondrinker when those around you continue to become more and more inebriated. Looking at my companions with a sober eye revealed new "after five" personalities that were not allowed in the office envi-ronment. The new personalities were willing to share their stories of unrequited love, dysfunctional families, and incompetent bosses. But without the truth serum alcohol, I didn't feel like participating in the ongoing conversations. Drinking was a vehicle for the airing of petty problems and without drinking, the problems seemed less important, especially since most of what was being said would be forgotten the next day. I became more and more removed from the conversation as my drinking friends reemphasized each issue or recounted each story with every round ordered. Being sober had its lonely moments, but at the same time, my solitude provided a new clarity.

By not drinking I was sleeping better, had more time and energy to work out, and felt an overall sense of well-being. During January when I went out for drinks with friends, I had little to complain about, which made for some lopsided conversations. I had stopped making excuses for not drinking, while others around me were making excuses to drink. I began to notice subtle changes in myself. I had little tolerance for talking about work once I had left the office. I became more productive in the office as a result of getting an earlier start each day. When my alarm clock went off, I was hitting the snooze button less and less. Without pesky hangovers in the mornings, I was able to arrive at work on time with my daily exercise already completed.

Since the average cocktail contains about 300 empty calories and each night out involved more than two or three drinks, it was easy to see how I became a little soft. Let's just say it, a 292-calorie piña colada will not only make you drunk, it will also make you fat. So now that I wasn't spending early mornings nursing hangovers, I no longer had any excuses for skipping my workouts. And without those extra calories, I was able to shed a few pounds in the process.

With my now slightly slimmer physical self intact, I began to seek more from my yoga class than just muscle-extending poses. My yoga teacher chanted, "Look to the beauty within, recognize your intentions, and be grateful for the teachers that have come before you." I listened and began to apply these principles to my sober life. A wise yogi, Desikashar, stated that "yoga exists in the world, because everything is linked." This lesson resonated with me in that I seemed to have come to a place where everything was beginning to link up. It would be extraordinarily out of balance to have more Ketel One in your bloodstream than actual blood while maintaining a perfect bow pose. So I woke each day with a new resolve, to act with intention and remain present. Falling off the local bar stool was not at all a good way to stay balanced in my new time of enlightenment.

Even so, once out of the yoga class where everything was pure and perfect, the need for a rewarding cocktail seemed a natural choice for all the good karma I was creating. My inner partyer was rearing her ugly head, aching to come out, sometimes even craving dirty martinis while doing downward-facing dog. How I would achieve my spiritual enlightenment with these rampant cravings remained to be seen. I became preoccupied with getting to February for a real celebration. Since the yogis were teaching me the lessons of balance in all aspects of life, I figured it wasn't very balanced to go without cocktails.

During the last week of January, I rejoined my girlfriends and their pretty cocktails. Their drinks looked like little Barbie beverages, fizzy and fruity and bubble gum pink. I would be lying if I said that club soda, even with a splash of cranberry juice, was providing me with much joy. I even asked the bartender to put it in a champagne flute, but it really did not help. I wanted a big girl drink.

As my friends moved on to rounds two, three, and four, they became more chatty and catty. I am sure that had I not been there they might have revealed some of my most trusted secrets. My sober presence prevented them from blabbing about my secret crush on the UPS man. Were these little pink drinks causing this open and, at times, ugly behavior? It was then that I began to call the drinks what they were, Evil Barbie Juice. All is fine with Ken and the pool party with one or two of these pink drinks, but have three or more and you turn into a head-spinning exorcist. The ancient Italians put it a bit more eloquently with the saying *"in vino veritas"* or "there is truth in wine."

At the very least, those around me were becoming more up front about their feelings; whether that was the inner truth coming out or the outer cosmopolitan going in is something I can't know for sure. However, I do know that that little pink drink unlocked some not so pretty things, a lesson that I noted for the future.

The most important lesson I learned from my month of alcohol abstinence was not that I drank too much, but that I needed to stand up to peer pressure from my fellow imbibers and drink only when I actually craved alcohol. When February arrived, I returned to having dirty martinis with friends. Like Dorothy in Oz longing for her life back in Kansas, I had missed those most of all.

Today, on some occasions a club soda is my choice of drink, and on others there is no substitute for my favorite, vodka and vermouth. Going forward, my social life balanced to create just the right mix. I have learned to speak up for myself both at the bar and in many other areas of my life. Being more comfortable with my decisions has made passing on a drink now and then more acceptable. Somewhere in my mid-thirties, I am learning to "just say no" and have the confidence to stick with it.

February

SHOPPING

He who knows he has enough is rich.

—TAO-TE-CHING, TAOIST PROVERB

Shopping is the museum of the 20th century.

—DALAI LAMA

I selected February, the shortest month of the year, to give up my single biggest vice: shopping. My account began in the 1990s, when retail sales were at an all-time high and the stock market was a safe investment. A wealth of good fortune existed for the American consumer, and my friends and I were no exception. We had elevated shopping to a literal boot camp, filling our weekends with trips to stores to check out the latest merchandise. Hours between meetings and lunches were ripe for "retail therapy." As Carrie Bradshaw so eloquently put it on the very popular *Sex and the City*, "Shopping is my cardio." Accustomed to busy work schedules and unusual work hours, we had to grab our fun when we could. For many of us, the local Giorgio Armani store provided just the right tonic.

It was a harmless addiction. After all, my college tuition was paid off, I was single, and I rented an apartment in nearby Hoboken, New Jersey, to avoid Manhattan prices. My credit card, which I paid off in full every month, was used for all purchases. I owned nothing and owed nothing, a phenomenon common among my circle of New York professionals.

The idea of purchasing something new for a special occasion was magical. What I failed to recognize was that every day was not a special occasion. For me, shopping became less about buying something special, and more about accumulation and consumption. I was becoming more than an occasional user purchasing a blouse, belt, or boots weekly. Expeditions to outlet malls and sample sales were social outings for my circle of friends. The constant bombardment of fashion magazines and television channels devoted to style convinced me that

I needed to keep up with all the latest trends. Visiting neighborhood shops was a requirement for fear that the salespeople might forget my name or that, God forbid, something new would come in and I would miss out on it. My prayers were answered when *Lucky* magazine arrived. It became my bible. "Must have" items would be put in a file for a future "scavenger hunt" through the wilds of Manhattan.

As with many women, my mom taught me how to shop. A day at our favorite shops followed by lunch was a grown-up girl treat that we would plan and look forward to weeks in advance. We were always looking for a certain item on each trip, which made our trips like shopping missions. My favorite memory was purchasing my first pair of designer jeans, Vidal Sassoon jeans, which I hustled through elementary school with.

For me, shopping was an outing, a social get-together. Much more than necessity, a trip to the store was a way for women to bond and to enjoy each other's company. At Loehmann's, for instance, how many times have you asked another woman's opinion on a dress you were considering buying? Shopping is a sisterhood. Television and technology mirror and exploit this trend. Oprah Winfrey's show about her favorite things is one of the most popular of the year. QVC and the Home Shopping Network have given birth to an entirely new breed of television watcher. And let us not forget the rise of e-commerce, which has added another outlet for people to buy products and services.

Those shopping trips with my mom comprised my "classical training." Visiting the local merchants as an escape from the everyday is the purist form of shopping, it is shopping as recreation. However, the new bevy of buying choices, embodied by the Internet, has made shopping accessible all the time! All of these choices have made my trips more productive. I could actually surf the net, 24/7, and review the merchandise before going to the store. If I wanted to keep pace with all the trends, I could flip on the television where our fascination with celebrity extends to fashion.

The choices offered to consumers today are not your mother's dress shop. Couple this with the outlet malls, which offer endless discount designer choices, and you have a country obsessed with purchasing. Buying fuels the economy, a good economy creates a stronger country, and so along we go. Although it is hard to believe that scooping up Chloé minidresses is an act of patriotism.

In January I received a phone call from my financial manager at Merrill Lynch applauding me on my savings over the last month. When I answered, "This is nice; my investments are really paying off," he probed further, "What have you done differently this month?" I meekly replied, "I stopped buying shoes." The evidence was overwhelming. My buying had become a knee-jerk reaction, done without thought or planning. This was in contrast to a lesson learned during a favorite shopping time, back to school.

I would get madly excited about the first day of the new school year not because I was particularly scholarly or in need of seeing my long-lost friends from the previous May. My motive was much more materialistic. I could not wait to get new stuff, specifically a big shiny red Trapper Keeper (a spiral notebook complete with a school filing system with multiple pockets). This desire, much like my unrequited love for Andy Gibb, went unfulfilled. My parents had a much different plan for the first day of school and, for that matter, the first week of school. My parents operated on the supply-and-demand philosophy of school supplies. Year in and year out, I hoped that this would change, but it did not. While all of my classmates arrived on day one with the full rainbow spectrum of school supplies, I had only a small memo pad. My parents' approach, perfected during fifteen years of sending kids off to school, was a wait-and-see game. Does it not make more sense to see what each class requires before you go buy (dare I say?) an unneeded notebook or pencil case? Turns out that my parents were right—a theme that continues alarmingly throughout my life.

This philosophy was now beginning to make sense as I looked at my closets, which contained tons of things that were not wanted or needed. With my new mind-set, I decided to come clean. "My name is Mary and I'm a shopaholic." Since admitting you have a problem is the first step, I was able to form a plan. The most immediate necessity was to put a stop valve on purchasing. Next, addressing the collection of clothing I had already amassed:

- Clothes with price tags on them
- Items that did not fit when I bought them and will never fit
- Special-occasion items for occasions that never happened
- Shoes that hurt my feet

- Items that did not go with anything in my or anyone else's wardrobe
- Items that are impossible to keep clean or wrinkle free
- Outfits that can only be worn to specific concerts from specific bands on reunion tours
- Extreme fashions that are neither fire retardant nor possible to get into or out of

The checkup call from Merrill Lynch forced me into the closet, so to speak. Calculating the figures on items that were not in my current wardrobe rotation totaled an astounding amount. I assessed what items could still be returned and brought them back immediately. Next, I established the two-week rule, if an item was not worn within two weeks of purchase, it had to go! This is a great rule to consider when buying any item. Make sure you are aware of the store's return policy. I learned this the hard way when accompanying a friend to a sample sale and proceeded to purchase more than $500 in non-returnable clothing and accessories. Currently, none of those "must have" items survived my closet scrutiny. That shopping session taught me that even though something is beautiful and fits perfectly, without an expressed need to wear that sequined skirt, you should not buy it. This epiphany gave rise to a phrase that my friends and I still exclaim whenever we are shopping together. We ask, "Where am I going in that?" and if we cannot come up with a valid answer, the hot pink velvet handbag goes back on the rack. The sample sale debacle was further proof.

Could there be deeper reasons why I was shopping so much? I wondered, Could my shopping weakness be a genetic flaw? I quickly discounted the idea of a hereditary gene that made me crave trips to the mall. Societal influences beyond my control held more weight. Americans are consumers that respond to advertising. The advertiser's objective is often to create a need for impractical items. Take the sports utility vehicle, for instance. Manufacturers design these vehicles specifically for consumptive reasons, including status or power over others on the road. They both create and feed into the mind-set that bigger is somehow better. Spend more money, buy more gas, and keep the economy rolling. This concept is prevalent in America's shopping society. Moreover, the tone is set early on by targeting young children, starting them on a lifelong path to consumerism. My childhood relationship with my Barbie dolls illustrates this point. The marketing of the Barbie doll with its endless renditions of the same doll smartly created a desire in little girls, me among them, to collect each and every one. And collect them all I did, even the most coveted, Quick Curl Barbie, which at one point had to be replaced because her hair had been "over-curled."

Even though I considered myself an independent trendsetter, I found I was still succumbing to my own form of peer pressure when the month first began. For example, if a colleague at work went shopping at her lunch hour, I would need to be involved for "purchase review." Purchase review is the act of examining and critiquing the newly purchased items with a group of like-minded shoppers. Sometimes this can be as fulfilling as the shopping itself. Externally, I would be happy for my colleague and her good purchases. Internally, I would be planning my next visit to the same store to make the same purchase. The desire to shop is a learned behavior. This comparison helped me to figure out the motivations behind why I shopped and to recognize the influence that advertisers and friends have on me.

I was constantly searching for a new and improved product: color-stay lipstick, teeth-whitening kits, and hair-thickening shampoo. How many times have you purchased the latest trend to make yourself over from the outside in? I buy the hype. As I flip through my old photos, I am alarmed to see the 80s trends most of all. Sky-high hair and ripped sweatshirts inspired by *Flashdance* gave way to the Joan Collins linebacker shoulder pads. Certainly the designers of today have contributed more to fashion than these examples, but they are good cautionary tales nonetheless. I shudder to think that the country's romance with retro will lead me back into parachute pants and cut-up sweatshirts. However, this might be a reality as I look around at the racks of hip-huggers and madras shirts at the mall.

On a recent trip to Paris, I observed many stylish women buying expensive high-quality pieces, like an Hermès scarf in a classic pattern. Later, after they had grown tired of it, they would trade it in for a new scarf at a secondhand or reciprocal store. Reciproque is a Parisian store with several locations across the city, each specializing in a different item, shoes, handbags, etc. In Paris, flea markets are very popular. They also carry major designer products. You can find Chanel, Prada, and Chloé for half the price if you can deal with wearing last season. *Mon Dieu!* That trip to Paris opened my eyes to an entirely new way of life. They have it right; they buy only what they need. My new credo is:

- Do not impulse buy. Create lists for what you need each season and then after you have shopped around, purchase. Walk out of the store and come back if you are not sure.
- Research every item. No matter what you think you need, it is important to consider what you will wear with each item as well as where you will wear it.
- If you purchase an item, be prepared to swap out another to accommodate your new purchase. This can be done by "gifting" the item to a friend or donating it to a local secondhand store.
- Save all receipts and apply the two-week rule. If you do not wear the item within two weeks, chances are you can get along without it.
- Do monthly reviews of your closet. Purge, donate, and consign to keep your closet tidy and enable you to get to your items quickly.
- Ask your friends and family for support to help you stop frivolous spending.

One of the most important lessons learned this month was that I did need help from friends and family who had previously enabled me to shop till I dropped. This lesson was never more apparent than this past holiday season. My friends and I had planned a get-together so that we could exchange gifts. We had worked hard to get a mutually-agreed-upon date on our calendars. After a series of e-mails, we selected a hip new lounge for cosmos and snacks. My dear friend swept in thirty minutes late proclaiming that if we ate and drank fast, we could still catch the Burberry sample sale. She was opting for shopping instead of sitting down with her friends to toast the holidays. She would not be able to pass an hour of time without shopping. Secretly, I wanted to take her up on her offer. However, I willed myself to stay and I began to see the frivolity of our shopping. I was embarrassed that I considered shopping to be a more viable option than spending time with my close friends.

In order to continue my evolution through the month, I decided to recoup some of my money through resale or charitable acts. I opted for a combination by becoming a consigner. Most every area has consignment shops for designer, vintage, or everyday clothes and accessories. Half the proceeds of the sales usually go to local charities and the other half comes back to you. This did help cushion the blow for some of my misguided shopping trips. In addition, there are several fantastic local charities, such as www.dressforsuccess.org, which provides clothing for underprivileged women entering the workplace. Putting things into perspective helped me to get a realistic grasp on my wasteful ways.

The lessons were beginning to take shape. Could I actually live a better life by shopping less? What seemed impossible at the beginning of the month became clearer. Too much shopping was taking up too much of my free time.

The biggest lesson was understanding the act of purchasing and purchasing big. A trip to BJ's or Costco is a good example. These stores tempt the shopper in all of us to buy larger and larger quantities of everyday products. On my last trip, my purchases included a gallon jug of stuffed peppers and thirty-two rolls of toilet paper, which required their own room in my apartment! These misguided purchases were made after calculating that 45 cents per pepper was a deal that could not be beat. As for the toilet paper, I seemed to be under some odd notion that I had better stock up in case there was a shortage on trees in North America.

Surely, stocking up and saving is generally a good idea, but perhaps this was taking it a bit too far. As I strolled down the gigantic aisle with my gigantic shopping cart, I completely embraced the bigger-is-better concept. Every time I approached a product, my mind would leap to one phrase, "But it's only . . ." "But it's only $8.99 for a thirty-pack of Milky Ways" or "But it's only $19.99 for an inflatable inner tube." This experience helped to guide me to a moment of clarity. I began to recognize that I was not buying what I needed. Instead, I was acting on an impulse created by the retailer, whose goal is to ring cash registers. These retailers did a fantastic job; they convinced me to buy things I did not need. Now when I shop, I go with a list of essentials to make sure that I stay on track.

Certainly choice is good, but having too many choices can create confusion. Sometimes eliminating the many choices from your world can make life much less stressful. Unfortunately, I learned this lesson in the most stress-filled way. Several months after my Costco visit someone stole my purse while I was having dinner with a friend. While the inconvenience was both time consuming and troublesome, the lesson was life changing. My purse contained my wallet, daily planner, cell phone, makeup, reading material, and sunglasses. I was devastated to lose all of these personal items. However, I was less upset about losing cash and credit cards than I was about losing all of my possessions. When you lose all of the things that you deem most important to you, life teaches you that you can get by with a minimum of creature comforts. Today, after replacing all of the items, I view them differently. I no longer try to assign emotion to these replaceable things.

In a society where advertising and the media are constantly persuading us to buy new products and have the latest in fashion, swimming against the tide was my way of getting in touch with my actual needs. It calls to mind the words of Helen Hayes, "Through the years I have found it wonderful to acquire, but it is also wonderful to divest. It is rather like exhaling."

This month gave me the feeling that going without is not so bad. I shop only when I need something. My entire attitude toward my needs and wants has changed. There is a distinction. I no longer shop to live and amazingly I always have something to wear.

March

ELEVATORS

*The American Heart Association lists
"taking the steps" as one of the top things to do daily
in order to achieve cardiac health.*

The old adage that March comes in like a lion and goes out like a lamb had renewed meaning for me as I opted to take the steps instead of the elevator this month. This was extremely daunting, as my job was on the tenth floor of an office building. Luckily, my apartment was blissfully located on the ground level. Since a neighbor I was friendly with lived on the fifth floor, and I handled his steps with ease, doubling the number of stairs to get to my office would not be a problem. In my endless preoccupation to stay fit, I figured the additional steps would increase my activity and help to burn off extra City Bakery brownies, the consumption of which might even necessitate an afternoon trip downstairs. This resulted in my body, mind, and appetite being in synch in an elevated state, often described by athletes as the zone.

Recently, a softball teammate had been sidelined from the zone with a knee injury. Her lengthy rehabilitation was a constant reminder of how we take moving our bodies without pain or injury for granted. Elderly relatives also made me notice this as they lamented their constant ailments. When they were my age, they would charge up those steps. Taking their meaning literally, I would take as many steps as possible while I was still young and able, because some day I would not be young or able.

Because guilt is one of the cornerstones of my genetic makeup, this wisdom became a mental pep talk for taking the steps. I envisioned the fantastic Knick Willis Reed entering Madison Square Garden in the 1972 playoffs hobbled by a leg injury. Even though he had a debilitating injury that would have sidelined any athlete, he summoned the courage to play and led his team to victory. If Willis could win the NBA playoffs on one leg, then I could get myself up a few flights of stairs every day.

Even though my office building was by no means a high rise, it always surprised me to see how many people took the elevator to the third or sometimes even second floor. With everyone relying on the elevators, it was not unusual to see the line often snake outside the building. And because machinery can break down, there were often only two elevators working at a time, rather than three.

My first mornings without elevator assistance were particularly interesting. The stairs were located beyond the elevator bank on the first floor, which required me to pass the entire line of people to reach them. Awe-struck colleagues initially watched in disbelief as I confidently strode by. Some of them thought I was cutting the line and began to get territorial, standing up straight or even creating a human roadblock of sorts to impede my route. This was particularly amusing, as complaining about work had become a phenomenon for many of those in line. Yet all of these people were hopping on the elevator and rushing to their desks. Were they all late? This phenomenon was apparent on subways, buses, and city streets as the grumpy workforce got into its daily routine. They might not love their desk jobs, but they would have knocked me down on their way to get there first. While my fellow employees were competing over who was first to get into the elevator, my own competitive streak was growing. I started to muster my strength for the challenge ahead. And like Rocky running up the steps of the Philadelphia Art Museum, I began to feel as if I were in training.

Many of my colleagues were alarmed that I opted to take the steps. As I worked in a small company, everybody knew me and that I was heading for the top floor. The line turned into cheering fans waiting to high-five me before the big game; they were Burgess Meredith cheering from my corner in the ring. With all this fictitious bravado, it was no surprise that I became cocky; cocky about my physical fitness, cocky about my discipline, and cocky about my individuality. Being bold and proud made me appreciate my entry into a smaller elite group. This elite group comprised three people: one who had a fear of elevators, one who was a fitness nut, and one who was too impatient to wait for the elevator. I was now relating to each of these co-workers, all of whom I never noticed taking the steps before. They were seeking their own benefits. The colleague who feared elevators claimed that he had always had a fear and a mistrust of the pulley system on the car. Add to that a healthy dose of claustrophobia and you have the human "StairMaster." He reasoned that the cables and pulleys were not stable enough to hold. Further Internet investigation on my part showed many studies reinforcing the relationship between his fear of elevators and claustrophobia. While I had ultimate trust in machinery for the specific reason that it had never failed me before, I was beginning to see his point. I was thinking about the idea of small spaces, in particular. My fear of small spaces was born and developed at countless general admission rock concerts in the 1990s. Not blessed with height, I would often listen to my favorite rock band while seeing nothing but the back of a Metallica shirt. I was no fan of being closed in.

Even though I was buoyed by my cheering section, the first- and second-week climbs followed a disturbing pattern: feeling great on floors one through four, a little more challenged on five and six, breathing more heavily on seven and eight, and get the crash cart out on nine and ten. It seemed implausible that an active person would be hyperventilating and wildly out of breath upon reaching the top floors. Apollo Creed had beaten Rocky, the Lakers had won the NBA finals, and I could not make it up ten flights. Glistening with sweat and bumping headfirst into my co-workers while trying to catch my breath was neither athletic nor professional. My cheering section had turned into a group of hecklers making the victorious walk of fame feel more like a walk of shame. More practice was demanded to conquer the big ten. Since stairs were everywhere, in malls, apartment buildings, and parking garages, training could take place just about everywhere. I had to retrain to avoid the more natural choice, which meant take elevator over steps, drive instead of walk, and make one trip instead of two. Awareness now was directed toward retracing my steps. According to Weight Watchers, where points are exacted for everything you eat, activity is emphasized as part of the plan; points are given back for exercising. Further support was mounting for the City Bakery brownie.

Increasing my overall activity was making each climb easier, so by the second week I was able to blurt out a "good morning" or two without too much heavy breathing. A giant step for this woman, if not a small step for womankind. The steps created a new awareness for physical activity. Often when working out at the gym, I would become bored by my routine. Many trainers recommend variety in workouts to achieve the best results. My new "StairMaster" was unpredictable. It demanded concentration and focus, which connected my thoughts to my actions. Consciously setting my own physical goals and achieving them was a lesson easily applied back at the gym.

By week three, I was beating my co-workers who took the elevator. On average, my co-workers were wasting five to ten minutes in line, sometimes even more. What they gained in impatience, I gained in energy and time.

To say that the benefit of this month was only physical would not reveal the entire story. While traveling the steps, I had more time to prepare for the day, review my schedule, and focus on daily goals. By nature, I'm not a morning person. It takes time for me to be cordial in the early part of the day. Leaving my home, taking mass transit, and then getting to the office after ten flights, there was little opportunity to talk on most days. "Small latte with skim" and "thanks" were the usual comments. Forced elevator chatter was no longer a pressure. Choosing to walk instead of ride offered more private time before the stress of the workday crept in. This private time had both mental and physical benefits. I had entered the zone. But it was not until many months later that the larger lessons of this month were realized.

I was visiting my office on a Saturday to pick up a few cumbersome items, which necessitated what should have been a routine elevator ride. Once I was on board, with the down button pressed, the doors came to a hesitant close. The elevator did not move and the buttons did not light up. The first ten minutes were by no means enjoyable, but I had convinced myself that the elevator would be moving in no time. During the next thirty minutes, my nerves began to set in. Impatience, indecision, and helplessness were soon to follow. The machinery had failed and the elevator was stuck in limbo between floors.

Very early into elevator purgatory, my voice and my fists tried to get the attention of the outside world. Luckily for me, a skeleton crew of building attendants heard my cries for help. I yelled loudly, as being trapped in the elevator for even a minute longer would make me irrational. Confidence was at a premium when the steel box began to close in. *Batman* episodes where the caped crusader and the boy wonder would physically escape from life-size vises came to mind.

After forty-five minutes, four men, and a crowbar, I was freed from my small prison. I quickly reached for a "lifeline" to dial to the outside world. As if all machines were in a conspiracy, my cell-phone light flashed low battery when calling the friend who was waiting for me. And while I had no way of knowing that this would happen as I traveled the stairs in March, this experience contributed to form my new attitude toward elevators and steps.

When looking back at the month, I had not realized how aware I had become of my environment, specifically the building itself. Each floor's entry points and emergency routes were in my peripheral vision every day. By osmosis or conscious choice, I learned my building's ins and outs. This was valuable knowledge.

On the morning of September 11, I, like most people in the country, embarked on what seemed to be a normal workday. As we know now, this was anything but a normal workday. As the facts became apparent, most of my colleagues opted to stay put until more information created a clearer choice. In a choice between fight and flight, I chose flight. Clearing off the top of my desk and sliding it into my tote bag, I left the office quickly, not considering changing out of my high heels to sneakers. Along with my friend and work colleague Dennis, I

took the stairs down the ten flights, never even considering the elevator, and was out onto the street in a matter of minutes. Although the elevator was working, I was
convinced that it would not work under the unknown
circumstances. The stairs were my choice; they were
familiar to me. I recalled from many trips up and down
the floors that had security key access and those that
had fire exits providing an alternate access to each floor.
My preparedness and awareness were a source of some
confidence for me on that fateful day.

Many months later, I was again at Dennis's door, this
time as a blackout swept the entire Northeast. Unaware of
exactly what was happening to Manhattan, we grabbed
our tote bags and, for me, sneakers this time, and once
again bounded for the steps to escape.

March's lessons were multifold. I began the month
simply to become more active. What I learned was to
be aware of your surroundings and that, unfortunately,
an emergency plan is a necessary part of everyday life.
I learned that I needed to identify fire exits and emergency routes, just in case. And while the world has
changed and unpredictable things can always happen,
what I know now is that a little preparedness can go a
long way.

April

NEWSPAPERS

A poem begins in delight and ends in wisdom.
—ROBERT FROST

The *New York Times* hitting the front stoop has signaled the beginning of the day for my entire adult life. Eager to see the new installment of the news, I would marvel that so much was going on in the world that it warranted a new paper every day. The newspaper was a present to be unwrapped, providing details of stories and events, information to process, and a clean crossword puzzle. This everyday ritual began for me in college, where I was a journalism minor. The *New York Times,* considered to be the paper of record, was required reading. Years later, I was still reading the paper

to find out *who, what, where,* and *when.* However, the
final tenet of *why* was suddenly elusive. These reading
rituals, like most things, are done routinely with little
thought or examination. As a result, something had
changed; reading in general had become mundane and
arduous. I was in my first reading slump. I was no longer
eagerly awaiting my morning ritual.

The new sections in the paper, Automobiles, Dining,
and midweek Styles, caused me to start reading between
the lines. The pressure to complete the entire paper had
become too much to handle. I had become a serial
reader. Since I found nothing to hold my attention, the
morning routine featured roaming from section to section, from newspaper to book, retaining little of what
was read.

Falling into slumps happens to all kinds of people
for all kinds of things including dating, working out,
dieting, and even shopping. I have weathered all of
them, including a short-lived hitting slump during last
year's softball playoffs. Usually, things return to normal.
However, this recent slump was showing no signs of
budging. Reading with discipline was rooted in childhood, when all books were read from beginning to end
without exception.

Every Saturday morning, my mother would take me and my three brothers to the town library. We would split up; Joe off to the mystery section, where he was systematically making his way through the Agatha Christie catalog, Matthew to the sports section, and John to his study of Native American history. In the early days, a kindly librarian read from a wide selection of books during story time. This was my first reading group. I remember the smell of the library, a mixture of old bindings and Jean Naté perfume, that permeated the giant staircase leading downstairs to the children's area, nestled on the lower level. Sitting on the floor listening to *Eloise, Amelia Bedelia,* and the *Little House on the Prairie* series, I marveled at the people and places in these fantastic tales.

As soon as I could carry them, the entire Laura Ingalls Wilder series would be toted home where I would read and reread each volume. The continuity of meeting Laura and Mary in every book was comforting. The pile of books checked out on Saturday morning would be read immediately, sometimes even in the backseat of my parents' Delta 88. By Tuesday afternoon, we would be back at the library for a fresh stack. This voracious reading habit continued throughout college with a curriculum of writing classes required for a journalism minor. Once I was out of college, reading was still fundamental and, ultimately, became my career.

This philosophy extended to the newspaper, where even the Sunday paper was completed with zeal, for fear of missing something. Recently, that zeal had been replaced with a dread of reading the newspaper for fear of encountering what seemed to be an increasing amount of bad news. This disinterest in reading had crept into all areas. Even the occasional bodice-ripper romance I squirreled away to read before bedtime no longer held interest. The motivator when reading as a child was a desire to discover something new. Today, reading much the same thing repeatedly was not providing anything new or noteworthy. It was time for a new writer. April as National Poetry Month created a natural change of reading material, one which I had little experience with. The poets would hopefully provide the literary jump start that I was looking for.

With recent scheduling demands, there was no time to read books at all. All of my reading time was consumed by hard news stories and the Metro section. Again, the pressure to perform by reading every article was apparent, rather than actually reading it with thought or absorption. It was as if I were waiting to be quizzed on the entire paper's contents. Even the weekend paper provided no solace. A colleague of mine insists upon reading the entire Sunday paper, even if it takes all week. Every day on his desk, in addition to the daily paper, is a section of the paper that he did not get to over the weekend.

Why were we all competing and exhausting ourselves to read this paper? One reason was simply to answer the ever-present water cooler and cocktail party question "Did you see the article in the *Times* today?" That taken literally can mean three things: First, you have the paper and have not read it yet, or second, you are a headline skimmer and did not really read the paper, or third, you were wrapped up in another section and have not gotten to the article in question yet. The answers would follow one of those reasons. Saving a nickel for every time this question was asked would have been a great savings plan. After the first week ended, I had lost count. I wanted to be the bold person who said, "I don't read the newspaper, I only read Whitman."

Putting the newspaper on vacation hold and replacing it immediately with Emily Dickinson was day one. I got out of bed and went to my poetry shelf. These few precoffee, preshower, precrankiness moments were designated reading time. "I dwell in possibility," I recited and stopped. Was there ever a more perfect headline than that? What does it mean to dwell in possibility? To be able to linger in a happy shade of gray where anything and everything was possible was appealing. This was a great start to the day. "I dwell in possibility," was a poetic pep talk of sorts. The words were other-worldly and led to a greater understanding of their meaning. It was like gaining admission to the most elite reading group and being rewarded with a new enlightenment.

The poem concludes, "The spreading wide my narrow hands to gather paradise." A smile had replaced the panicked grimace to finish the paper. The day began with an entirely new outlook, different from all others, a day where exciting possibilities existed. Immersed in the morning, the mundane routine returned. However, that day felt a little lighter, a bit happier; I let the day begin differently with a beautiful poem that resonated in my life and was beginning to dwell in my own possibilities.

Within that first week a dilemma presented itself. Well-meaning friends had decided that a technology loophole would help me to stay on top of things during the information breakdown. It took only a slight pause when an article arrived by e-mail from www.nytimes. com. I was a reluctant subscriber, not yet reading the paper online, preferring the messy newsprint on my hands to hitting computer keys. Truthfully, navigating the access codes and user names was still something of a problem. It was a relief to press the delete key on the computer when this electronic substitute arrived with the morning mail.

Week two continued with the works of the major poets. Walt Whitman was a repeat performer. "I contain multitudes" is one of the best lines ever written. As the week progressed, the ethereal poetry of Christina Rossetti became the top story. Her work was a wake-up call for the senses, demanding to be read out loud, something that demanded a slower pace. This was a marked change from rushing through the morning news as fast as possible. Rossetti's poems were methodical and perfect to read out loud. The ones about nature in particular were usually lighthearted, playfully describing toads, grasshoppers, and frogs, none of which shared my urban landscape. I had not read out loud since elementary school when Mrs. Barto would make me and my fellow second graders recite passages from one of my favorite stories, *Dinosaur Ben*.

Looking at my newspaper habit more closely led to an overall review of my reading in general. I moved from poetry to fiction to nonfiction. There was little space in my apartment for anything else besides books. At one point, nearly seven hundred books lined the bookcases in every room. Creative ways to pack books, such as stuffing them in drawers, in kitchen cabinets, and in closets, became the norm. This expansive collection included first editions, advance reading copies, paperbacks, most of which were signed by authors I encountered through my job. Most book lovers are the same way; the more they read, the more they want to add to their collection. They have a hard time letting go.

Inevitably, bibliophiles designate a growing collection of books as a "going to read" pile. Unfortunately for me, that reading pile had long remained untouched. A friend recently took me through her bookcases. Her "going to read pile" had turned into an entire room! She reads constantly and will probably get through most of them, but an entire room devoted to "someday" seemed a little excessive. In April reevaluating my relationship with reading extended to perceptions about the books themselves. A good indicator was the vast number of volumes that were primarily eye candy. On the shelf sat a full set of the Pocket Poets, which were coveted for their beautiful packaging. Each poet had a different-colored book jacket with a coordinated ribbon marker creating a kaleidoscope of color. The set collected over the years was in pristine condition because the books were never opened. They were judged only by their covers. After all, who had time to read poetry? There was little time to stop and smell the roses or, much less, to stop and read about smelling them.

Even though I was enjoying my morning reading, which helped me to escape to a new literary world, there was still the problem of how to answer "Did you read the paper this morning?" coupled with the problem of having no one to talk to about my morning reading. I considered stopping the conversation dead in its tracks with, "No, morning is for poetry only." Needless to say, I was the only one in my office who was choosing the major poets over the Metro section, despite my efforts to start a poetry reading club.

One morning, stumbling over a copy of Elizabeth Barrett Browning's *Sonnets from the Portuguese,* I discovered one of my favorite passages:

A False Step
Sweet, thou hast trod on a heart
Pass; there's a world full of men;
And women as fair as thou art
Must do such things now and then

The title of the collection, *Sonnets from the Portuguese,* may seem off for a poet of British descent. Robert Browning had referred to Elizabeth as his "little Portuguese" because of her dark complexion. This collection was written by Elizabeth and intended for Robert. I could not have scripted a better page six romance.

What seemed to be missing from my daily reading was the immediate interaction that surrounds reading a newspaper article. Reading had always been a solitary act, especially where novels were concerned, but the newspaper was different. Feeling left out of conversations by the water cooler was becoming more and more frequent. Talking about what was read was as important as the reading itself. If a bear reads the paper alone in the woods and has not discussed the headlines, has he really read the paper at all?

In need of conversation, I decided to join a reading group. Included in the group were people with different personalities, political backgrounds, and tastes. The group was initially meant to talk just about the literary selections. The resulting discussions immediately involved much more than that. Apartment searches, engagements, pregnancies, and new jobs were all discussed. As we focused on the literature at hand, the issues in the book would springboard the conversation into a group therapy session of sorts. Was life imitating art? Our conversations were always lively and interesting, even though at times we needed to get off the couch and return to the book.

The group dynamic provided the interaction that was missing for me. Now, in a group of diverse people who had different views, there were at least two sides or more to every story. This interaction became even livelier when it was time to select a new book. Five people agreeing on a book to read is not an easy task, and was further complicated by the fact that we all had very different ideas about what a reading group should be. Most members were looking to escape into fiction and discuss themes and language. Because of the hard news deficiency, current affairs, biographies, and even history were my suggestions.

Ultimately, we found a happy medium. The first

selections were as diverse as the group that picked them and included contemporary fiction, history, and biography. At the time I'm writing this, we are reading a lengthy tome about Franklin and Eleanor Roosevelt that had to be divided into two sessions. Not surprisingly, my title selection combined the reading group with news. History won out.

Additionally, the reading group and morning poetry had created more focus for reading comprehension. Genuinely interested in the topics being read, I no longer bounced from page to page. Reading was fun again. Starting the day with poetry instead of bad news had lasting effects. Keats's and Browning's voices would visit throughout the day, offering a welcome distraction at times from the office routine. In the true spirit of expanding beyond the news, my appetite for reading more diverse literature increased.

As a result, the "must read" pile became a priority. *Walden* by Henry David Thoreau became a part of week three. Sampling a bit each day replaced the structure of reading from beginning to end.

When Thoreau was asked why he had decided to live apart from society, he answered, "I went to the woods because I wished to live deliberately, to front only the essential facts of life, and see if I could not learn what it had to teach, and not, when I came to die, discover that I had not lived." Thoreau took gentle notice of the nature and beauty that was Walden Pond. My exploration was decidedly less drastic than moving to a self-built home in the woods. However, I was beginning to take notice of my own gentle surroundings. With Thoreau's approach, I appreciated the subtle beauty of what was around me; the Manhattan skyline at night, the pink dogwood trees on my block, and the brownstone-lined streets of Hoboken provided their own poetry. Most of all I saw the beauty in taking time to read, to find my own Walden Pond in each day.

April was a month of teaching an old dog new tricks. Even though reading was and is a part of my life, trying new things like reading poetry out loud and joining a reading group helped to create a renewed appreciation. The reading group in particular gave an outlet for conversation, something that was lacking without discussing the newspaper. Did I miss the *New York Times,* the *Daily News?* At times, but for the most part, the variety of new material taught more about exploration of myself than any newspaper ever could. Without the newspaper every day, choosing historical biography or current affairs became more of a welcome option and challenge for me. Reading about history gave me a new perspective on today's events, in which I often found parallels and similarities. I now read the *New York Times* with a different perspective. I put less pressure on myself to finish the paper and only choose certain sections to read. When asked if I saw the article in the *Times* today, I answer truthfully. Sometimes I have seen and read the article, sometimes not. My answer is always the same: "Tell me about the article." Usually, the reader is looking for the interaction and connection that reading creates, the same interaction I discovered among my reading group. This month led me to the knowledge that reading, discussion, and history go hand-in-hand.

Poetry reading created a slower pace that allowed me a new awareness of my surroundings. There was time to smell the roses. Thoreau became my unlikely companion along the way as I embraced my new mantra, "Expect the unexpected." As for my apartment with books lining the floors, walls, and shelves, a more minimalist approach to "book keeping" has been adopted. I read off the "I am going to read that pile" first. I vary my reading list to include reading group selections, and nonfiction, and I always visit the poets who started it all.

 May

CELL PHONES

Everyone is talking, but no one says a word.
—"NOBODY TOLD ME," JOHN LENNON

Wireless bill $127.50
Monthly service charge $31.74
Home airtime charges $82.80
Monthly minutes 686

Strangers talk to me all the time, so it was not unusual when in the ladies lounge at Bloomingdale's I began to answer a fellow shopper who had started up a conversation. Even though the lounge was empty, I quickly realized the woman was not talking to me. She had taken her cell phone into the stall to continue a chat that even nature could not put a stop to. As the woman put a final flush to the conversation, I noted the places technology has gone, literally.

How many times had I heard people say, "What did we ever do without cell phones?" The quick answer was, we didn't know what we were missing. The long answer is a series of more questions. Was everyone punctual back then? Did people miss appointments? Were we more efficient? This month, I vowed to hold the cell phone hostage to see how much I would be missing.

My preparations began in earnest. I reset my service so that my cell phone would forward all calls to my home phone, ensuring that no phone calls would be missed. The message was simple: "You have reached the cell phone for Mary, this phone will not be used for the entire month, if you want to talk to me, please call . . ." With that done, the phone was stored in a dresser drawer, where it would remain until June 1. The next conversation was with my boyfriend, Frank. It described a detailed plan for his moving day, including rendezvous points and an elaborate backup plan. With such preparation, my lack of wireless connectivity would not be a problem for him. Or would it?

The day of the move began routinely. After completing my morning workout, I noticed no blinking light on my home line. Since parking is hard to come by in our neighborhood, the first leg of the master plan involved moving my car to secure a place in front of his apartment. After the spot was secured, I returned home, where my landlines would put me a phone call away. Unfortunately, the new phone line that had been installed to accommodate a cable modem earlier that week was not working. This fact was made clear to me much later and rather emphatically as Frank circled the block speed-dialing all of my "available" numbers. The master plan had been foiled in the first hour. If the home phone had been hooked up properly, this confusion might have been avoided. But having a cell phone with me at all times would have provided a much needed backup.

My first lesson was a lopsided choice: Be more clear with my directions or refine my extrasensory perception. After the move was completed, dinner with friends at a nearby restaurant was a plan that should have been easily accomplished. Picking a place for dinner and meeting there on time did not seem like an insurmountable task. Without the cell phone that held my friend's phone number, the degree of difficulty for this task increased. When our friends called my boyfriend's phone, I lunged to pick it up. "Foul!" he cried. The month was meant to have no cell phones and that included all cell phones regardless of their ownership. When would the confusion end and the tranquillity begin?

I know a woman so attached to her cell phone that she would place the phone between us every time we met so she could not only hear the phone ring, but also see the phone light up. As if watching a fireworks display, she would giddily grab the phone with the designer ring. The universally accepted excuse was not given as she repeatedly answered the calls. Unfortunately, whoever was sitting across from her at the time was supposed to marvel at the phone as if it were a newborn. Feeling second best to a cell phone was not a good feeling and one that I vowed never to have again.

Free will is part and parcel of cell-phone use. It is easy to ignore the cell phone and complain about it when you have the power to turn it off and on. Screening calls at inopportune times from inopportune people is empowering. When the phone is taken away and, along with it, your options, being distracted starts to look better and better. Even though I had called

Jennifer the night before to tell her about our dinner plan, we had yet to confirm an exact time and meeting place. Our friends commonly practice the art of making noncommittal plans. Getting out of things last minute as a fallback position was a given. "I am going to be at a meeting and can meet you at five or six or why don't I just call you from my cell when I'm done." I had uttered this fail-safe phrase countless times. Knowing that I had this in my back pocket afforded me endless choices: showing up late, putting off making a commitment to meet, and of course the last-minute cancel. The old adage of "At least she called" could always be relied upon.

Luckily, that night Jennifer had Frank's cell phone, where she was able to reach me but not directly. After being reprimanded for using other people's cell phones, I put a new rule in place. To make this month work, amendment one would prohibit access to all cell phones, not just mine. As a result, a series of missed messages and calls led to an unwitting game of hide-and-seek throughout our neighborhood's bistros. It seemed that relying on someone else to pick up the cell phone on your behalf also had its pitfalls. Answering your own phone messages is one thing, but juggling my calls with his proved to be disastrous. The next day, we realized we were in the same place at the same time. The cell-phone ban was setting off an explosion. May 1 resulted in standing up my boyfriend and driving my friend crazy in a wild goose chase. My simple life seemed more complicated than ever. How would I get through thirty more days?

One night, when running late for dinner, I inadvertently left the directions and address to the restaurant at home. Part forgetfulness and part habit, I had always relied on the cell phone at the last minute to obtain directions or information.

During that cell phone–free evening, none of the helpful features were an option. My option was wandering around for nearly fifteen minutes before I recalled the "old-fashioned" way of being lost, which was stopping to ask for directions. A nearby shop owner told me unequivocally the restaurant's address. She was unequivocally wrong, which necessitated another ten minutes of circling the block until the location was found. My phone, or "Little Yellow" as I referred to it, was much more efficient. Without my fingers doing the walking, everyday tasks that were once performed effortlessly required more thought and double the effort.

Not connecting with the über-helpful cell-phone operators was something I could get used to; getting lost and relearning basic skills was quite another. Little Yellow was more than a tool to keep me up to the minute with my friends; it also held all of their personal information. Home, mobile, and office phone numbers for all the people in my world were locked inside.

Confession number one: I consulted the phone address book to acquire numbers. Just to play fair, the actual call would be made from my home or office phone, enabling me to not breach my service agreement. On these occasions, the message signal would go off, as people had left messages despite my outgoing message. Those messages would be left until the end of the month. It was one thing to retrieve information, it was quite another to retrieve a wireless message. Amendment two allowed for the occasional number check. Amendment three was to ignore those messages. If those calls were important, the caller would find me another way. Perhaps other people might consider giving up the wireless as well, although I doubted it. The temptation to reprimand those callers was far more tempting than the notion that an emergency call was locked in wireless limbo.

The wireless world became a club that I no longer belonged to while all of my friends and family did. It would have been easier to make a list of people who did not have home phones than people who did not have cell phones. More creative solutions were needed in the coming days. Those around me were being turned into personal assistants as they were directed to each other for updates on my location. This game of "Wireless Waldo" often followed the same routine with a script that became familiar with the friends who were required to answer for me. "Mary is unable to take the call right now, but she wanted you to know that she will be at the pizzeria at 4:30 if you could meet her there." The justification was that the cell-phone ban could not be responsible for everyone's mutual need for staying connected. The return call seemed less viable when you made others call on your behalf. In many cases, this seemed to be the only way for my friends and me to avoid tripping over crossed wires.

In my abstinence, those around me using cell phones became more prominent, making me hypersensitive to usage. Not only did everyone have a cell phone, but it also seemed as if they were using them more and more. People crossing the street were talking to their friends, in the Laundromat a man tried to reach his office, school kids on the block were going wireless, and the phone was even ringing in church. While at the supermarket, a young woman consulted her husband about what kind of salad dressing he would prefer for dinner. I am a patient person, but when I bumped into her again in the ice cream aisle asking whether he would like chocolate marshmallow or rocky road, my good nature dwindled. Some of the best examples of phone usage came from people on the job using time to dial up. The cleaning lady at the gym or the bus driver on his route are using their minutes wisely.

My paddle against the technological tide was stacking up to be a wipeout. The ban was in dire straits when my hot rod 1989 Honda Prelude was added to the mix. At 185,000 miles, never was there a car more in need of emergency roadside assistance. The Palisades area of New Jersey is tough terrain for any car. Driving my car in this area is the equivalent of racing a go-cart on the Indy 500. As the Prelude lumbered down the hilly roads, speed began diminishing. At one point, the car may have even moved backward. Unaware that my gear was stuck between drive and overdrive, I was stuck between panic and hysteria. In an unfamiliar area with no way to call for help, my AAA membership was useless. It turned out that my panic, like my cell phone for that matter, was misplaced. After correcting the shifting mistake, the little lemon regained cruising speed at thirty-four miles per hour. Amendment four allowed for cell-phone use in old Honda Preludes. The phone would be carried with me in case of an emergency outgoing call for help. The little yellow phone in its pink polka-dot holder resumed its rightful position next to all its coordinating accessories in my purse. It felt good to have the accessory family reunited. Life without the cell phone was one thing, but life without the proper accessories was quite another.

The world was a wireless Wild West where everyone but me had a phone. Virtually all of them had phones that failed to include manners on their calling plans. There were as many offenders as there were ring tones. Without the phone, there was more time to sit in judgment and note violations.

The things that people did seemed outrageous. I was no exception, as a few months back I inadvertently left my cell phone at a friend's house. As I routinely continued a call when leaving home, the bulky cordless landline phone was placed in my book bag. Such was the dependence on chatting on the go. This gaffe came to mind as I vowed to become the new Emily Post of cell phones as of June 1. Making creative use of my quiet time, I began to categorize the type of user I was and the type that I encountered.

The first and most obvious offender is the loud caller. While one is riding on the bus, a one-sided conversation is overheard because it is impossible to shut out the volume. She says, "Yes, I am on the bus now." "Yes, I am on my way to work." This commentary usually indicates that the cell-phone user has just left the presence of the person on the other end. Somehow the play-by-play becomes necessary. And like most play-by-plays, an audience is needed. More often than not this was on the 126 New Jersey Transit bus to New York City. In college there was a roommate whom we called "the reporter." She would often go from room to room announcing her actions. "I am getting an apple out of the refrigerator now" or "My laundry is done." I would bet that she is a cell-phone user of unparalleled proportions and a natural for the 126 bus.

Another caller I love to hate is the caller who has no personal boundaries. Some of the conversations I have overheard have made me blush. Do these callers simply wait for public venues to talk about their most intimate issues? Words to the wise: Unless you are certain that your boss, your best friend, or your spouse is not in the immediate area, it is probably best to be discreet. Some conversations require privacy.

And of course my personal favorite, the cell-phone sleepwalker. The caller who is so focused on their conversation that they move in a weightless, gravity-free zone where they refuse to be distracted. In most cases, this kind of singlemindedness is appreciated and even rewarded. However, in this case, this skill is downright unsafe. Neither car nor truck nor fear of night will keep this caller from their cell-phone rounds.

Cell-phone usage can be contagious, which brings me to our next offender, the continuous caller. This person makes call after call after call, usually while sitting next to me, who is undoubtedly reading at a coffee shop. These types of callers generally have no ability to commit to or make a decision on where to meet and when or with whom for that matter. Their plans necessitate a flurry of phone calls to firm up plans. Truth be known, I was guilty of that as well, making frequent calls simply because I could. Now a decision needed to be made and committed to. Making those extra calls only added to confusion and indecision. The commitment of nonwired life was demanding. Talking the talk was easy enough, but walking the walk was quite another thing. As time passed, my hope was that this task would become easier. Instead, relationships were being put to the test.

That classic saying of only hurting the ones you love applies to this next situation. I was delayed on the phone with a computer repairman when call waiting clicked in. In my rush, I told my boyfriend that I could not talk. The phone call ended, leaving me only a few minutes to make an appointment with the repairman. Grabbing my bag, I ran out of the house leaving my lights on, thinking that the nearby appointment would be brief. When forty-five minutes went by and I returned home, I noticed my boyfriend peering into my apartment window. "I can't talk" was the last thing he had heard and then he had not heard from me for almost an hour. My lit apartment made him assume that I had likely either been taken hostage or had fallen and could not get to the door. This night turned me into "the reporter," updating people where I would be at all times. The luxury of using a phone when on the go or in between appointments was no longer available. Instead,

I would make a plan and stick to it. Perhaps the month could allow a "couples only" cell phone similar to the sporty red phone like Commissioner Gordon's on *Batman*. This way I would know when Frank was calling and be able to answer only that phone. This seemed like a viable option for our relationship to get through the remainder of the month. My status as "the reporter" became increasingly important after that incident.

Learning how to stick to a plan became my modus operandi. When making lunch reservations, friends would be told to call in any messages to the restaurant where we would meet. Most people did not question this at all, assuming malfunction or service interruption as the excuse for not having a mobile phone with me at all times. Either you can't hear the phone ring or messages are time delayed in some manner. And the constant ringing can be annoying. With all of its faults, I still missed "Little Yellow" terribly.

I narrowly missed a nervous breakdown when a woefully late bus delayed me for thirty minutes when I was meeting a friend. Again, fate stepped in; I did not make the call and ended up arriving first at our meeting point. There seemed to be nonchalance in my life at this point. This was a new situation; I have always been overly punctual. My college friend Maria was always late. "Maria time" was generally one hour later than the original meeting time. We learned to set our clocks accordingly. She explained the reasoning for her tardiness as twofold. Not only did she have no concept of how long each task would actually take, but also that she had unnatural distaste for waiting. Until this month, I was her polar opposite. This role was played reluctantly at first until midmonth when it became more natural. This made for a new type of confidence. Now I was realizing that I had more time than I thought and that the world would not end if I was not the first one there. It was okay to be late, I thought.

This month's deprivation caused my boyfriend to nearly reconsider our recent engagement, jeopardized friendships, and created unbelievable confusion. Those were powerful messages to be learned by becoming unreachable. The initial reactions were a mixture of confusion and disbelief. Everyone around me claimed that it would have been impossible for them to have given up the phone. They, like most people in the world, had come to rely on the phone on a daily if not hourly basis. Even leaving an outgoing message on my cell phone telling all callers that this phone would be rendered inactive for a month, still required further information. Giving up the cell phone was completely out of the ordinary. My own lessons involved the dependence placed on the phone to achieve the simplest of tasks. Scheduling meetings and appointments in a world that is more often unpredictable than not, made holding to commitments nearly impossible. Instead, the spontaneous would be avoided. If a friend was unable to be reached by the time I was out of my home phone's reach, I simply would not make plans with them. The "give me a call if you are in the neighborhood" way of life was no longer available to me. All shades of gray were lost in my black-and-white world. Most of my hours were spent close to a landline, my freedom being held hostage.

The ability to exist with minimal comforts in a creature-comfort world is a challenge worth attempting. Like going to the dentist or eating your vegetables, living without a cell phone is something I might be happy that I did, but would not want to do again. The lessons gained this month gave me an entirely new appreciation for the cell phone. Now able to determine the necessary from the unnecessary calls, I rely on the phone to avoid being late or uninformed. Last-minute calls to friends to meet for coffee are as much a part of life as being delayed in traffic or misplacing directions. These are all viable excuses for using the cell phone. However, relying only on the cell phone for these tasks creates an imbalance. On the last evening of the month, my boyfriend was flying in from London and would be arriving while I was out to dinner with a friend. After his being away for a week, I could not wait to hear from him. Holding my commitment to go without the phone on this night made for a very uncomfortable choice. This predicament exemplified my challenge all month. Do I leave my home phone and possibly miss a call or do I live in the moment and carry on with a plan? In the end, I went out to dinner and called my boyfriend from a pay phone. My metamorphosis had come full circle.

With two days left in the month, my brother called Frank's cell phone to double-check on tickets for a game they were to attend the next day. They had trouble hearing each other. Inadvertently, the phone was handed to me to decipher the final plans. I picked up the conversation and dropped the abstinence, not realizing my mistake until hanging up. Those in the room were now shocked by these seemingly routine actions. Even after thirty days, my instinct to pick up the phone had not changed.

Again, getting away from my own cell phone was easier than getting away from all cell phones. Even the final day provided a challenge as a traffic jam derailed me from making an appointment. Since I was determined not to be detracted from my goal, a pay phone became the only answer. It was as if I were using a phone in a foreign country. After several redials, the local phone call was able to be placed. Just for the record, the cost of that call has more than doubled since the last time I used a pay phone.

When the calendar page turned to June 1, I flipped on the phone, sent out an e-mail update, and picked up a few hang-up calls on my cell phone message service. On the first day back to wireless land, I received only one incoming call and made no outgoing calls. Perhaps everyone around me was finally trained to reach me in other ways, or maybe, now that the flip phone has been flipped on, I have already begun to take it for granted.

DINING OUT

I was 32 when I started cooking; up until then I just ate.

—JULIA CHILD

Money spent on breakfast and lunch $65–$75
Sushi twice a week $30 per meal
Weekly ATM withdrawals $200
Weekly total $330

Considering the high cost of my meal plan, I knew I could get back to basics and could do better on my own. I would have to find room on my full plate of a schedule to prepare lunch and dinner. A busy life relied on getting food on short order. This month, the schedule would be rescheduled to include good home-cooked meals.

I was beginning to notice the other toll this lifestyle was having on me. When eating dinner out, I would be served what would be enough food for three or four people. Granted, if it was my grandmother's cooking, I would certainly muscle through, but this kind of volume eating caused me to unwittingly gain fifteen pounds over the course of a year. It was time to get hold of myself, literally. Coupling these epic proportions with my childhood lesson of finishing everything on my plate was creating a dietary double-bind. I was being presented with supersized portions and feeling the pressure of becoming supersized me. This year I was going back to basics. I would maintain my weight through diet and exercise. Moderation in all things was my mantra.

Up until recently, home-cooked meals had always been a big part of my life. With four mouths to feed, my parents rarely took us to restaurants. Dinner was an opportunity for my mother to display her skills as a fantastic cook. This family talent began with both of my grandmothers. Each was born in Italy. "Nana in Plainfield," my father's mother, was born in Basilicata, where she specialized in big Christmas Eve fish dinners. "Nana in Montclair," my mother's mother, was born in Sicily, where she perfected her deep red tomato sauce. I recall going to my grandmothers' homes for major Italian meals that lasted the entire afternoon, beginning with appetizers, then pasta with meatballs and sausage, then a roast with potatoes, and finally dessert, fruit, and nuts. The table was crowded with traditional dishes that became "Italian-Americanized." My grandparents took pride in their American status and wanted to blend into their new country.

During my college years, I would visit my grandmother in nearby Montclair for some of her home cooking. She always made copious amounts of food. I suspected that she would make the same amount regardless of how many guests she was expecting. To be sure I would not offend her; I ate every bit of what she served me—usually macaroni or manicotti or some other Italian treat. On one occasion, my grandmother "Na" announced with her thick Sicilian accent that we were having "chicken chow mein"! I was a little shocked to see a mound of fluffy white rice and browned chicken with celery arrive in front of me. We all still wonder how she made that dish. It was a few simple ingredients:

chicken, rice, celery. It remains the best chicken chow mein that I have ever had.

The Italian tradition of cooking with simple fresh ingredients is a lesson that I brought to my own kitchen. Somehow in the hubbub of my busy career I replaced those basic ideals with takeout. Now, how to find the time!

Since I needed some help in time management on the household front, I thought I would go to the master, my mother. Her system worked for our large family, so I figured it could certainly work for just one person. In an attempt to organize our lives and the kitchen, my mother assigned each day of the week a specific meal. Sunday was always macaroni with gravy, a thick meat sauce. Monday was generally soup—lentil, pasta e fagioli, or escarole. Oven-baked chicken with mashed potatoes, beef Stroganoff, and pasta carbonara were all choices for Tuesday through Thursday. On Friday, whether it was Lent or not, it was always fish. I would roll up my sleeves and help my mother bread flounder fillets that she would lightly fry or bake. The side dishes were standard as well: baked macaroni and cheese with several kinds of cheeses including ricotta; stewed tomatoes or broccoli rabe would round out the plate and add beautiful color.

Her Sunday meal needed the most preparation. We would awaken on Sunday to the smell of meatballs frying in olive oil. Next, the meatballs would be added to the fresh tomato sauce. On the Sundays when my mother would make baked dishes, like lasagna, stuffed shells, and eggplant or veal parmigiana, she would assign each kid a role in the preparations. I was usually chosen to grate the mozzarella that was a staple for all of the baked dishes. I would drag my feet to the kitchen for my assignment. Layering the lasagna or eggplant was the most coveted task, one that I would not graduate to until years later. Grating was done by hand with a square grater held over the bowl. There was no food processor in those days. Two to four pounds of mozzarella was the normal amount. Depending on the dish, one of us would also have to bread the eggplant or veal cutlets. Those of us who woke up early enough would be recruited to roll the meatballs or help prepare the beef bresaola that were both staples of the meaty tomato sauce.

After the kids had prepared all the components of the dish, my mother would assemble the countless layers of pasta, cheese, and sauce. The sauce or gravy was homemade. My mother would can bushels of tomatoes in August in advance, a chore she still does today. In fact, during the canning season, it is hard to get into my parents' house without having a cascade of tomatoes roll at you from the kitchen. The shelves in the basement are lined with hundreds of Mason jars filled with the tomatoes that would be the base for sauces for every Sunday that year.

This on-the-job training should have come more into play when I was preparing my own meals, but I chose to take the easy way out, often by taking myself out. Lunch in particular had changed for me. In elementary school, I refused to eat lunch at school with the other children. There was something about the sterile cafeteria atmosphere that I could not handle. Luckily school was close enough that I could get home to eat lunch and return in plenty of time for the afternoon session. Every day, I would feast on leftovers such as manicotti or a meatball sandwich. The notion of a hot dog or peanut butter sandwich was alien to me. I remember complaining to my mother, who thought that I should try to eat with the other kids, that their lunches did not look good. I further explained that looking at the peanut butter and marshmallow fluff sandwiches made me lose my appetite. Today, ironically, I love peanut butter so much that I can't even stock it in my house. I could eat an entire jar in one sitting. I never did, however, develop a taste for marshmallow fluff.

My grandmothers and mother had unwittingly created a food snob. My love for food even steered my vacations. I would plan yearly sojourns to Tuscany. Before going to Italy, I would prepare by getting down to my eating weight, which is five to seven pounds lighter than normal. I wanted to eat with reckless abandon while on vacation. And I always did. I adored going to Florence for sightseeing, shopping, and, of course, gelato. I would often have it twice a day. I loved that Italy still observed the siesta. What could be better than enjoying a big Italian meal and taking a nap before returning to the workday? I wished that my lunch hour back at home could be as fulfilling. If I managed to get out on my lunch hour, I would often choose to go to the gym. A brown bag lunch became a necessity. Few people seemed to be eating anywhere but at their desks these days.

There was one man who dined out every day. He would often invite other executives from the office to join him. His philosophy was that people should sit down to eat a nice meal each day. On one occasion,

I was dining with him at a lovely outdoor restaurant when two vice presidents in my company rushed down the street with their brown paper lunch bags. They had dashed out of the office between meetings to grab a quick lunch before the afternoon meeting schedule began. The man I was having lunch with was no less busy than the two brown baggers. I remember his words, "Don't you feel sorry for them? They don't know what they are missing."

A few days into the month, I discovered Whole Foods, a mecca of fresh foods not far from my house. They even have foods that are already prepared. On my first visit, I bought the makings for pad thai after studying and inquiring about the ready-made version at Whole Foods. I went around the store and picked out all the necessary ingredients. It was relatively easy to make and delicious. I took home a sample to my mother the following weekend, and while she did refer to it as that "spaghetti you brought me the other day," she seemed to enjoy it.

With the success of the pad thai, I decided to further improve my culinary skills. Even so, I was not fully prepared to end my romance with restaurants forever. What I wanted to break was the food-on-the-go addiction, where I ended up sacrificing taste for convenience. I wanted to bring the quality restaurant experience home and regain my passion for food.

My daily routine of coffee and muffin and turkey sandwiches had sapped my tremendous passion for good homemade food. My repetitive habits had bored my palate. It was time to jump-start my day. Luckily, my office had a kitchen equipped with a microwave on the floor where I worked. I started bringing a packet of oatmeal each day to heat up. I would also bring a piece of fruit, so now not only was I skipping the high-calorie muffin option, I was eating more healthfully too. Planning my breakfast helped better control how much I ate. Planning my meals also eliminated choice, which was becoming a problem for me. The muffins and pastries were a temptation, as well as the pizza and burgers for lunch. I could happily avoid those with my own meal plan. I even opted to prepare my own salads, as I was easily spending $12.00 a day on a calorie-loaded salad bar concoction. The notion of spending $12.00 on greens made me lose my appetite. I could do this at home. And so I did.

I reported to the kitchen for an inventory session. To say that the cupboards were bare is putting it mildly.

My refrigerator contained a large jar of hot peppers, salsa, and Gatorade. Not exactly a tasty meal. And the fact that I kept little food in my apartment made eating out the only way to eat at all. I needed to stock up on the essentials for the weeks to come. My plan was to eat smaller portions during my three meals a day. I avoided snacks unless they were fruit. To make life easier, I would put a big bowl of fruit on my desk as the week began. I brought cheese and dairy back to my diet. I favored beans and rice for burritos and chili, fresh vegetables for salads, and pasta and chicken for dinner. I took special care to buy items that I could prepare in advance and freeze. Like my grandmother and mother before me, Sunday became my day to cook big. I would prepare easy meals that I could take with me all week. Veggie chili was the easiest and most inexpensive and became my first favorite. I would stir up a big vat on the stove, store the chili in containers, and freeze ten at a time.

Before work I would get a plastic container of chili out of the freezer and I was good to go. I could sprinkle a little cheese or sour cream on top and grab a flour tortilla on the side. This is my favorite lunch, a great way to gain energy and something to look forward to in the middle of the day. In addition to tasting good, the chili helped me get more vegetables into my diet. It also did double duty at dinner, as a side dish with rice, a topping for quick nachos, or as a burrito filling. Now, instead of eating my lunch on the run, I was able to get a portion of good food that kept me on track fiscally and physically—as opposed to buying lunch and being presented with a gigantic portion of food.

At lunch one day, while waiting for a burrito to be served, I picked up a fashion magazine. On the cover was a story about the ever-shrinking Hollywood starlets. The obsession with these women getting smaller and smaller seemed to be contrasting the American obsession that bigger is better. I was about to eat a burrito that could easily serve six of the Hollywood starlets. It was no wonder that people were having food issues. America is statistically getting bigger, unfortunately, not better. According to the American Obesity Society, approximately 127 million Americans are overweight, 60 million are obese, and 9 million are severely obese. These numbers, like most of our waistlines, are getting bigger every year. People have become obsessed with food and weight. This in turn has led this fast-food society to look for fast solutions to its problems. And so the fad diets promising quick fixes have captured our collective refrigerator.

From Weight Watchers to Jenny Craig to Atkins to South Beach, it seems that almost everyone is doing some sort of diet fad. Creative dieters have come up with hybrids for all. My brother, for example, is a Weight-Watching Atkins type. I had dabbled as well. I even went without dairy foods for a year after a well-intentioned friend told me that it led to arthritis and a host of other medical problems. That diet did not sit well with my mother, who began making her Italian favorites sans mozzarella. She would say, "This is especially for nondairy Mary." The first time I ate pizza after that experimental year, I was doubled over in pain and had to lie down for the rest of the evening. These extreme diets were not working and were beginning to take a toll on my body and mind. Preparing my own meals all month reinforced the obvious lessons: Use fresh ingredients, control portions, and you will eat better, save money, and more important, feel better.

Now that I was having a domestic renaissance, I started to notice that I was not alone in the nesting craze. I had many new companions. The Food Network and the Fine Living channel were as obsessed with food and wine as I was. Four-star chefs doing tutorials in my living room became a major source of my own gourmet and home-cooked meals. I became obsessed with watching all the programs, especially *Easy Entertaining with Michael Chiarello* and *Paula Deen's Home Cooking.* Both of these programs seemed as nourishing to me as any meal. Plus I had taken to stealing my mother's monthly subscriptions to *Gourmet, Bon Appétit,* and *Cucina Italiana* for further inspiration. I was becoming a knowledgeable home chef. Special-occasion meals now became everyday meals made for friends and family.

I was feeling confident about my cooking prowess, so much so that I started to think that I could actually bake. My confidence grew after visiting a strawberry festival and I bought some of the bright red berries. I decided to make a strawberry pie. I couldn't find a specific strawberry pie recipe, so I consulted a basic recipe. Simple ingredients once again made for delicious results. I believe that everything tastes better with butter, and this pie was no exception. I saved a piece not only for my own mother, but for my boyfriend's mother, and they both responded favorably. It was official, I could actually bake. When I was invited a week or so later to a dinner party at the home of Frank's sister, I volunteered to bake the pie. Instead of strawberry, I would bring peach this time. Peaches are a lot heavier than strawberries and, being a novice baker, I had not accounted for the change in weight and liquid. I was about to understand that such subtle shifts can make major differences. Nor had I accounted for the transport of the pie. I thought a foil pie plate placed flat in the bottom of a shopping bag would be sufficient. I did not realize that a warm pie needed proper support. In the end, the bottom literally fell out from under. I presented a bag of pie to my future sister-in-law. Luckily, I was able to bring a back-up dessert of pastries from my local bakery. You can only imagine my embarrassment when Maria served the sloppy mess alongside the pastries. Everyone claimed the ugly duckling pie was delicious, if not beautiful. I was mortified. This became an ongoing family joke when for Christmas last year I was given a ceramic pie plate.

I would not be truthful if I didn't tell you that I missed eating out at restaurants. I love the experience of dining out, being waited on, and all this accompanied by wonderful food and a great glass of wine. I learned about the restaurant atmosphere during my college years and after. I loved the buzz of the kitchen and the energy of the bar. The food service business taught me everything I know about time management and dealing with the public. The restaurant where I worked was a pool house, where a team of waiters and one food runner would split tips. On many nights, I would work in the kitchen, where I would run armloads of plates to tables for an entire shift. My kitchen roles also included that of the expediter, the person who would make sure that the orders were getting out on time and that the preparations were correct. In a busy kitchen, this job is imperative. I enjoyed having the run of the kitchen. The nights working in the kitchen were my favorites because I loved working with the chefs and watching the food being prepared. Sometimes they even let me shout out the orders. All of these experiences combined made me feel at home in any kitchen.

Because I loved restaurants so much, I wanted to replicate the experience at home as much as possible, particularly for special occasions. I began to notice that my improving kitchen skills were being appreciated by those I cooked for. A seafood risotto, which took months to perfect, is a favorite of my family and friends. Once you master patience, this dish becomes easy. You stir and watch and stir and watch. I make several versions of this risotto now, including asparagus and wild mushroom. Since Arborio rice is a creamy, substantive grain, it makes its own thick sauce. I never add cream to this dish. Even though the dish is the ultimate in comfort food, it does not have to come with all the calories. It just feels like it does.

I had improved my skills so much that my mother was even inviting me to cook with her in her own kitchen. This time, I was not the prep chef. I had the run of the kitchen now! Finally, after years of grating all of that mozzarella, I was taking the top job. Getting together with my family and planning the meal had now become a major part of our visits. We would compare notes on what we were making each week. Because my mother and I are both food obsessed, our first words to each other on the phone are did you eat yet and what did you have? We are always looking for new ideas, new ways to cook, and new ways to share our experiences together. The kitchen had brought people closer. And now I was beginning to bring people together with my own traditions.

This month started off as an experiment to try something new, to regain some interest in food after losing control of my appetite and my wallet. What I found was that not only was I spending a ton of money on food, but I was not enjoying my food at all. The lessons that I had been taught in childhood and later in the restaurant business were applicable to my life today. Food brings people closer together. I think one of life's greatest joys is to prepare a meal for those close to you.

July

TELEVISION

According to the A. C. Nielsen Company, the average American watches more than four hours of TV each day (or twenty-eight hours per week, or two months of nonstop TV-watching per year). In a sixty-five-year life, that person will have spent nine years glued to the tube.

Going without television is not a revolutionary idea. I know many old-school New Yorkers, especially those in the literary world, who do not own a television set. The few that do don't get cable. It is, however, very unusual for me to go without television. I have loved television my entire life. Tuning out this month would reveal just how much I truly relied on it. Truth be told,

I was not just a major TV viewer, I was also a channel surfer. Despite the fact that there are hundreds of new cable channels covering a never-ending host of topics, there simply was nothing on. Like life, TV offered too many choices. From the cereal aisle in the supermarket to the multitude of menu choices at my local diner, I was experiencing information overload. Watching TV became a constant occupation with flipping back and forth between multiple programs, coupled with the television being on at all times in all rooms of the apartment. Television ADD turned downtime into an endless bombardment. My fascination with finding out what else was on was hindering my ability to actually relax. I was convinced that there is always something better out there.

During my self-induced hiatus from television, I was out to dinner with a friend who had just gotten Tivo, the latest service that allows you to program in advance all of your favorite shows so you don't miss an episode. This revolution in TV technology had changed his life and he was looking for converts. He was awed by the fact that one of the dinner guests who was in the television business did not have this new modern convenience. My TV executive friend replied, "I don't have Tivo, I have a life." These words sounded off like a starting gun for the month.

Choosing which month to abstain from the tube was easy. During basketball season, I could be found glued to the set watching every New York Knicks game. The Knicks' failure to make the playoffs resulted in my choosing July to abstain from any form of viewing pleasure. As a lifelong Knicks fan (a condition for which I am currently being treated), I was required to watch every game, win or lose. As July was firmly planted in the post season, there was no risk of missing any Knicks games. I love the team so much that often I would watch the TV and listen to the radio simultaneously so as to get as much play-by-play coverage as possible. After a disappointing season, turning off the television should have been a blessing. I was able to avoid watching the L.A. Lakers dominate the NBA finals.

July began with my vow to have more serenity and less distraction in my home. I should clarify that I was avoiding watching television, DVDs, or videos, and refraining from watching at others' homes as well. And while I could not control when the TV was on at a bar or restaurant, I vowed to do my very best to walk away whenever possible.

Abstinence brought attention to the reliance of the creature comforts of my life. My TV habit was daily, watching every day without fail. On some nights, that might mean up to three hours of solid viewing. It was automatic for me to turn the set on upon entering the apartment. The drone of the evening news or *Jeopardy!* provided company in an otherwise quiet house.

As a child, I would plead with my parents to stay up later to catch the latter end of the Tuesday night lineup. *Happy Days* kicked off the night at 8:00 P.M. followed by *Laverne & Shirley*. In those days, my TV intake was limited. Bedtime was nine o'clock every night with no exception. When I was old enough to stay up a bit later, I was able to see *Three's Company* at 9:00 P.M. followed by *Taxi* at 9:30. Because my parents had set limits on my viewing hours, I felt a sense of deprivation. My lifelong love of television began as forbidden fruit.

During the 1970s and 1980s, I was treated to all of the original runs of the shows that now seem incredibly nostalgic. It was both exciting and sad when all my childhood favorites were being featured on classic television segments. And while there is something rewarding about seeing the favorite shows of your youth make a comeback, it is also depressing to realize that your childhood was so long ago that it was now considered nostalgic. I was certain that shows like *Charlie's Angels*, *Starsky and Hutch,* and *The Jeffersons* were goodies, but I wasn't quite prepared to classify them as oldies. When retrospectives about entire decades began to air nightly, I was further upset by the realization that the 1980s were twenty years ago. My days of playacting as one of Charlie's beautiful crime-fighting angels were over. It was time for me to put away not only my Members' Only jacket, but also my remote control.

In the interest of full disclosure, in addition to the three hours of television I was mindlessly watching at night, I was also watching TV in the morning, specifically relying on the network morning shows for news, weather, and light entertainment. My morning viewing would begin as soon as I could find the remote, which was usually somewhere in the vicinity of the bed, depending on where it had landed the night before. I would often fall asleep with the television set still on. At nighttime, after watching a few hours of television in the living room, which is a mere two feet away from my bedroom, I would prepare for bed. By turning off the living room set, getting under the covers, and then turning on a smaller TV set in the bedroom. From there, the program that was airing would lull me to sleep until awakened by a late late late movie that usually involved an alien invasion of a major city. A scramble to locate the remote would ensue, eventually putting an end to the offensive program. The remote would then mysteriously land under the bed, under the nightstand, and on one occasion across the room. So as not to appear completely addictive, my bedroom set did not have cable. After all, I was not a fanatic; I could go without cable in one room in my house.

Part of my journey this month was to be as honest as possible in terms of what TV meant to me. And in doing so, I have a confession to make. While working out each day, I was timing my midday miles to coincide with soap operas. I was running faster and farther with each week because I was returning to the gym every day to watch *Days of Our Lives*. The plot had not changed in years. "The stories," as the women in my family would refer to them, provided a familiarity and comfort to me. I could always rely on the fact that the villains would never change and that the good girls would soon turn bad. This cycle was like the ebb and flow of the tide. During my midday workouts, I noticed that I was not watching alone. At one point, everybody in my row of treadmills was hooked on the show. Some of the men were reluctant at first. When entering the gym, I would immediately ask the trainer to change the channel settings. Because I am respectful toward my fellow gym mates, I would always ask those on surrounding treadmills if they would mind the channel switch and none of them ever did. They were watching too. They reacted to the far-fetched tales, gasping and sometimes chuckling when appropriate. The slinky soap stars also kept our focus on why we came to the gym in the first place, to burn more and more calories. The summer season was very motivating.

Even though some of the plots may seem unbelievable, it is in this suspension of disbelief that my true joy of television exists. These shows provide total escape. No matter how much time has passed between episodes, the stories welcome you back in. They are a forgiving partner.

I could deal with no television in the morning or forgoing the soaps at the gym, even ignoring the tube at local bars, but what would I do with my evenings without TV? How would I get my news? For my journalism minor in college, daily newspaper reading was a requirement. Recently, I had lost interest in the daily paper and preferred to get my news as I sat passively on the couch. Things were going to change this month. It was back-to-school time, in a sense. After a few days, my eagerness to read the morning paper returned. And with the Internet, more online headlines could be found at my desk over morning coffee. This lack of the tube no longer distracted me from my daily preparations. I was now out the door with newspaper in hand in record time.

The morning dilemma was now solved, but what of the nocturnal challenge? Usually, after preparing dinner, I would head with plate in hand into the living room in time to watch a sitcom or drama from beginning to end. Cooking was timed around a certain program's start time. Rarely would dinner at home be anywhere but in front of the set. My kitchen table had become obsolete; the couch had taken its place.

In those early days of July, the mind games began the minute I would return home from work. I had to consciously challenge myself not to turn on the TV set. Turning on the radio for background noise helped make dinner preparations more tolerable. With music on, I would go through my evening routine: returning all of the misplaced items back to their homes, gathering ingredients for dinner, and finding reading material that would occupy me for the rest of the night. The challenge was staying busy enough to distract my mind from the set.

I continued spending time wandering around the apartment, trying to come up with tasks that would take my mind off television. This habit of TV watching was so ingrained in my daily routine that the excess of free time caused by not watching was overwhelming. Claiming that the day was too busy to get everything done, I was now experiencing quite the opposite. I had no idea how to deal with the additional time on my hands. The phrase "Be careful what you wish for" echoed in my mind. It was difficult to stay focused all of the time; TV was a way to unwind without thought. This must be why the expression "boob tube" became popular. It was much easier to fill my evenings with passive viewing than to actually use my time more productively.

I soon decided that the only way to keep my promise not to watch TV was to assign myself tasks each night. The weather was nice enough to go out for nightly walks after dinner. These leisurely neighborhood strolls were followed by a few hours of quality reading and then bed. On the few nights where the weather did not permit a walk, I would clean my apartment and get ahead of chores that were normally reserved for the weekend. Dry cleaning, bills, and laundry became a source of inspiration in getting me away from the couch. With a few extra hours each week, I now approached the weekend with a sense of completion. In a like manner, my entire workout schedule was also now completed before Saturday, making the weekend focus more about pleasure and less about choices.

Even though I was saving valuable time and organizing my life, I really wanted to see what I was missing on the set. The channel surfer in me was clamoring to get out. The water-cooler conversation involving what everyone watched last night left me with nothing to do but fill up my water glass. And while it could be argued that more of my colleagues would ask if I had read the *Times* op-ed page that morning than had I watched the latest reality show, I still had an urge to participate in the conversations.

At the time, reality television was just beginning to dominate the American psyche. At a house-warming party midmonth, I was completely left out of a conversation about a new series that everyone was watching called *Survivor.* This show was a total mystery to me.

The guests bandied about phrases like being "voted off the island" and "alliances." I had missed the birth of this entirely new breed of television. As the country continued to be made over to be made better, I was working on my own makeover project at home.

Even though I watched several nightly news programs, the result was not becoming more informed. Television watching was a way to get information, but that was simply not the case. My parents without cable know more about current events than most do. Anytime I need news on any topic whether local government updates or what starlets wore on the Oscars, my parents will have the answer. They are my own video clipping service. Their reputation continued when my work as an events manager demanded appearances on television. At that time, this was the only way that my friends and family could locate me. If they ever wondered where my travels were taking me, they need only switch on the entertainment shows or the eleven o'clock news and there I was standing next to an actor, politician, or athlete who was on a publicity tour. Instead of sitting in front of the television, I was the one on television.

My nonviewing lesson came into focus when a friend called me to plan a long weekend camping trip.

Up until that point in my life, my only experience of the great outdoors was via the Discovery channel. Without a second thought I immediately agreed to the trip. Other parallels seemed obvious. Watching television was a substitute for taking action. Instead of going on the camping trip, I would watch a wilderness program; instead of trying a new recipe, I would watch a cooking show; instead of reading a news article, I would flip on CNN; and finally, the ultimate in inertia, I would watch television to see the weather forecast instead of stepping outside.

Going without television for a month was not easy. Sometimes the need to unwind without thought is the perfect remedy to a mentally challenging day. While it may be tempting to do so, taking a passive seat on the couch is not a healthy life choice. I am certain that when I have advanced to an age where I look back on my life, I will not wish to have spent more time in front of the television. Today, I combine my viewing hours with everything else in my life to achieve a balance. Although it is always jarring to take yourself out of a tried-and-true time slot, the ratings can improve. I still indulge in the stories, whenever I can, but in smaller doses.

I envision all the places in the world that I enjoy that do not have television. The spa is my number one choice. Now I create my own home theater with a place to meditate, scented candles, and soothing music. No longer in need of distracting my mind or filling up the apartment with noise, I relish the peace and quiet. The disconnection from the set enables me to have a haven instead of a house.

August

TAXIS

"You talking to me?"
—TRAVIS BICKLE, TAXI DRIVER

New York City is one of the best walking cities in the world. Hordes of tourists arrive each year to walk the streets of SoHo, the Upper West Side, and the Village. One need only arrive in the theater district on a Wednesday matinee day to become enveloped in foot traffic. Working in the city every day should provide me with enough knowledge to navigate local streets. Sadly, this was not the case when a group of Central Park tourists asked me for directions. Suddenly, this fast-talking urbanite was at a loss for words. The head of the group asked, "Metropolitan Art of Museum?" Despite the order of the words, their question was understood. Most New Yorkers would be able to provide quick, clear instructions or at least point in the general vicinity. Instead, an awkward back-and-forth ensued, perhaps attributable to a language barrier, but the truth was harder to admit. Having no idea how to get there without the aid of a local cabdriver, I was without direction, literally.

The tourists were under one of the many universal misconceptions about New Yorkers. They assumed that I actually knew where things were located. Having grown up in the suburbs of New Jersey, it took a few years to perfect the city stare, city strut, and aloof sense of city indifference. Happy to be part of this thriving city, I found it hard to adopt a stern face despite the well-meaning advice, including my mother's simple instruction, "Keep your head down, look mad, and no one will bother you." This might have kept me out of danger, but would do nothing for the awareness of my surroundings. In all the time I spent in New York, the look was a guise for my malfunctioning inner compass. There were, of course, certain questions I could answer. When in my neighborhood, I did a fair job of helping stray tourists to navigate shops and streets that I passed every day on the way to work. My cursory directions were never very specific. The response would be something like, "Oh yes, there is one on Sixteenth or is it Seventeenth near the park, all you do is go over three and down one. You can't miss it." These highly specific instructions worked only in my neighborhood, where it is hard to tell that you cannot distinguish north from south or east from west. You can take the girl out of the neighborhood, but don't expect her to find her way back without her trusted taxi.

As far as misconceptions go, there are many about New York City taxis as well. Like, why during a beautiful spring day are there no cabs around at rush hour? Experienced passengers know that hailing a cab at 5:00 P.M. is nearly impossible due to the 4:00 P.M. shift change and the collective workforce demanding cabs all at the same time. If you are traveling downtown, a convincing argument might persuade even the most reluctant driver to make you his last fare. Many fear the cab, thinking that a cabdriver will take you for an unexpected ride. Even though my walking directions are not the best, I am aware that traveling from Wall Street to Broadway does not include a loop around the park.

But the biggest misconception is the idea that you

should not have a conversation with the cabdriver. Despite the glass divide between us, there has always been an opportunity for enlightening conversation, including news, sports, and, on more than one occasion, astrology. The cabdrivers' ability to report on up-to-the-minute news is a result of the endless talk radio they listen to while driving. Cabdrivers are city scribes who, when coaxed, will give their perspective on American news that is often interpreted through the opinions of their native lands. One astute driver once commented during the Clinton-Lewinsky scandal, "Why steal one goat when you can get ten goats?" His seize-the-day philosophy could be applied to my giving up taxi travel this month.

When I first started working in the city, I was afraid to travel in any other way. The habit of "grabbing a yellow" was the easy choice. Cabs run twenty-four hours a day, seven days a week, and offer routes that trains and buses do not cover. Besides, the subway system was foreign and complicated. Walking was time consuming and confusing without a map of the city or the trains. The endless cross streets made up a maze too hard to figure out. Some might consider asking for directions, but pride would not permit such inappropriate city behavior. Wandering haphazardly, appearing to know where to go, was the preferred choice. As with many things in life, looking the part was chosen over acting the part.

The desire to look the part and act the part contributed to my decision to stop hailing cabs. Sure, I would save money skipping taxis, but I had a nagging feeling that my mode of travel was holding me back from enjoying all the city had to offer. Gaining enough knowledge of unfamiliar neighborhoods and learning the city streets were enough impetus to force me out of the backseat.

Now that I was ready to brave the streets and the underground, cabs would be exiled for alternate means of transportation. My goals were to navigate the subway system, explore new neighborhoods, and learn enough to help the occasional tourist find their way.

Whenever setting out on a new experience that involves physical activity, it is important to have the right equipment. This became clear within the first few hours of day one, a beautiful summer morning made for petal-pink shoes with three-inch heels. Confidently gliding out to work, my sling backs parked themselves at the bus stop. A delayed bus and the birth of a blister on the back of my foot should have provided adequate foreshadowing. Determined not to fail within the first few hours, I completed the morning commute without any serious effect on my physical or mental state.

That day's lunch appointment, normally a carefree cab ride away, would now require navigating the subway system. My newly acquired subway map indicated that the F train was a few blocks away from the office and a few blocks away from the restaurant, requiring a bit more walking than I had bargained for. The sling backs not withstanding, the midday August heat seeping in and a wait on the subway tracks were contributing to a less-than-pink demeanor. Arriving twenty-five minutes late, unable to blame traffic, my confession said it all. The appropriately named F train takes longer than originally thought.

Later that night after arriving back in Hoboken, I found myself staring at the cab line or the bus line. On an uncomfortable shoe day, I would normally be on the cab line faster than you can say "paraffin pedicure," but today that was not an option. I noticed the cost difference for bus travel and taxi travel is roughly $3.00 to $4.00 each way depending on tip. By the end of the week, the pedicure would be a treat, as the weekly taxi fund was socked away for a newly created pampered foot fund.

It was clear from the first day that my shoes were not made for walking. A quick scan of the summer collection included coral sandals with pointed toe and high heel, black slides that pinched my toes before leaving the house, and one pair of loafers that could be worn for an entire day without injury. Filed under "what was I thinking," there was a recent purchase of high-heeled calf boots that were two sizes too big. To make them fit, two pairs of gym socks needed to be worn. When reviewing my collection, I realized that my shoes fell into two categories: sitting-only shoes for use in restaurants and mall shoes for use when shopping.

I spoke with a friend who had her own shoe categories, as she had designated an entirely new category, "cab only shoes." She treats her feet well, something worthy of emulation. When asked by a friend in one of those self-disclosure games that usually run along the lines of "if you were a vegetable, what kind of vegetable would you be?" I was asked, "What is your best feature?" Without blinking an eye, I said, my feet! Open-toed shoes and pedicures are a mainstay of my lifestyle. So with all this foot attention, it seemed implausible that so many bone-crunching, blister-causing shoes were in my wardrobe. I realized at that instant why this was so—I never walked anywhere. A change would need to be made to stop hurting the ones I loved.

I headed to the Short Hills mall in search of shoes that provided comfort but did not look orthopedic, still not convinced that I could become a shoe changer or even a cab shoe changer. Images of New York in the late 80s reminded me of women commuters who wore *Dynasty*-like suits with "slouch socks" and Reeboks. They too were shoe changers, donning spiked pumps to complete their retro 40s-cum-80s punk-suit look. With that image flashing before me, the comfort shoe section was approached with little comfort. After much deliberation, two pairs of kitten-heel shoes with ultra cushion were purchased.

Week two began with an uptown party during a torrential rainstorm that was hard to weather, especially without a cab or umbrella. It was one of those unexpected summer storms, best appreciated when sitting on a big porch near the beach in, say, Savannah, Georgia. The joy of the summer storm notwithstanding, the walk from the subway proved disastrous, even after purchasing a recently marked-up street umbrella for $7.00, having haggled the price down from $10.00. With the wind whipping and the umbrella immediately turned inside out, all hope of staying dry disappeared. Arriving at the party, I immediately ordered a dry chardonnay and waited out the storm.

Now that the first week's initiation blisters had finally healed, slinkier sandals were given a second chance. This time, I would be prepared. Pausing briefly at the local drugstore preventive medicine was just what Dr. Scholl's ordered—foot cream, moleskin, Band-Aids, and rubber insoles. Not surprisingly, these devices provided only a Band-Aid of solution. The shoes that "just need to be broken in" were an intricate design of style without substance. It was hard to believe that the tiny thong toe strap could inflict so much damage. The constant slapping of the shoe on the bottom of the foot combined with the pressure on the uncomfortable meeting between big toe and little, challenged both equilibrium and threshold for pain.

At a midday standstill, three carefully hidden Band-Aids made crisscross patterns on the top of my right foot. Wearing more Band-Aids than shoe says a lot about your character. It shows that you can withstand pain for fashion and that you also lack enough common sense to change your shoes when you have bled through several bandages. It also shows that either you are too busy to recognize pain or that you are too fashionable to succumb to it. In any case, this unforeseen fashion injury caused me to hit the inevitable rock bottom. With reluctance, I opened my gym bag and found socks and sneakers, which I wore for the rest of the day. Could the road to maturity also include not caring what I looked like?

With a newly developing sense of self, the cab foot dilemma seemed to be sorting itself out. Getting to and from work and navigating work appointments by train was at times troublesome, but with more planning, not impossible. All seemed fine until week two when my boyfriend returned from a weeklong business trip. I had made a dreadful miscalculation. The majority of cabs that I took revolved around my relationship, not my job. Not living in the same town presented transportation problems, as we were constantly shuttling back and forth to our apartments or to restaurants.

Even though his Jersey City apartment was across the street from Hoboken, literally, the cab fare is $2.00 more. If we had the cab drop us on the south side, safely on Hoboken soil, we would pay $3.00. If the cab dropped us on the north side, technically Jersey City, we would pay $5.00. This stunning display of math and greed still confuses and offends me. Our quick math revealed nearly $60.00 a week spent on cabs. To me, math always defied logic, but there was no confusion about these numbers. Taxi fares at $240 a month translates to $2,880 a year! Since most money conversations inevitably lead back to shopping, which inevitably leads to shoe shopping, this windfall was easy to apply to the pampered foot fund. Instead of continuing to blow money on taxis, we made an investment in bicycles, something we had wanted to do, but had put off for a long time. Logging a mile each day once or twice a day would make us physically fit as well as more fiscally responsible. Proving once again, why walk when you can ride? Not riding a bicycle since childhood, I found navigating city streets to be challenging, especially at rush hour and on the main streets. With a little more practice, we found alternate routes. Our favorite weekend activity became exploring the newly constructed bike paths on the Hudson River and enjoying a picnic lunch, which we would pick up along the way. We were rarely using our cars at all, preferring biking for errands, dinner, and travel to each other's apartment. After a couple of weeks of practice, I was able to balance a backpack lunch and carry a small beach chair on the ride.

Keeping to the schedule in the earlier part of the week was much easier than later. Much like those Monday gym workout people, anything could be achieved on a Monday or even a Tuesday and this month was no different. As the week continues, even best intentions can be challenged by the nearing weekend, where often "the wheels would fall off," so to speak. Thursday evenings in particular exemplify this weekend warrior attitude.

On this particular Thursday night, dinner plans were made on the newly hip Lower East Side. Streets like Allen, Rivington, and Stanton are still unfamiliar to many New Yorkers. Unfolding my trusty subway map, I noted the stop a few blocks away. I armed myself with a map, MetroCard, and book to read along the way.

My fellow subway riders donned a multitude of outfits. One man wore a knapsack and hiking boots, looking more suited for the Adirondacks than Midtown, a working mother juggled her briefcase and diaper bag, and a contractor in overalls hauled his tools along for the ride. We were united in our subway demeanor, an odd combination of apprehension that falls somewhere between church and prison. We all, however, shared one thing, sensible shoes.

Even though I now looked the part, I still had trouble deciphering the front of the train from the back. This coupled with my poor sense of direction often led me to the wrong street entirely. Above ground, as confusion set in, Dr. Phil calmly whispered in my ear, "Smart people ask for help."

Spying a lady taking her small daughter for a walk, I asked for directions to the restaurant. She was in full possession of that New York compass that I coveted. She gave perfect directions, including past the green deli sign and, once again, "You can't miss it."

Arriving at the restaurant early, I sat at the table and waited for my fellow diners. The first, late because she was taking a taxi and the driver could not find the address, and the second, delayed after walking the wrong way once out of the subway station. Perhaps the Jersey girl in me was not the only one afraid to ask for help.

After dinner we continued with a drink and more conversation. Before we knew it, it was well past midnight. On any other night, those of us that lived in Hoboken would take a cab across the Hudson. This shared trip would often top $50.00. After a long debate about our cost versus convenience, the group decided that the best way to travel was together, by taxi. It was not until all four of us piled into a cab that I realized how many times per month I paid this $50.00 taxi ride solo.

Late-night cab rides had been curtailed and the daily cab expenditures were eliminated, but my knowledge of the city had not increased more than traveling to work and the occasional lunch or dinner. It was time to force myself to explore new territory with a self-guided walking tour of Manhattan.

To get to know New York as a resident-turned-tourist, I made the Metropolitan Museum of Art my first stop. This was, after all, the direction that befuddled me when the month began.

My first walking tour included Central Park and the boathouse for lunch with my boyfriend. As a nostalgic trip, we toured past the renowned Dakota apartment building, which fits prominently into my favorite quintessential New York book, *Time and Again,* by Jack Finney. In the book, the character travels through time back to the precar 1800s. Like the character in the book, I cupped hands near my face to block the cars from sight, looking at the city through the same lens. The buildings appeared as if nothing had changed. Taking in the architecture and the look of a city was something I had really only done on vacation in a foreign city. New York demanded the same attention.

For me, this part of the city was rarely charted, as most of my time was spent near Union Square. After walking for hours in and around the museum and across the park, we opted for a relatively new New York phenomenon, the pedicab, essentially a person riding a bicycle that pulls a covered cart. We quickly realized that we would have been able to walk faster than the rider was able to take us, although it was interesting to view the city on bicycle, even the backseat of one.

Traveling New York is forever changed as a result of this month. Subways and walking have replaced the cab almost completely. It is on a rare occasion that a cab is warranted: at times late at night, at times during inclement weather, and at times when carrying too much. But more often than not, the MetroCard and comfort shoes are my current choices. Today, I am still reaping the benefits of function over form. A friend paid me the ultimate compliment for my well-protected feet. She had read about a foot beauty pageant and insisted that I take part. I accepted the compliment, but declined the contest, signaling the end to judging my feet only on their appearance.

No longer intimidated to ask for directions and cross streets or consult a map, finding a new way has become easy, especially when lost in Greenwich Village, where endless winding streets change names from east to west. Walking the area made me aware of these subtle differences.

The value of traveling by train or by foot is not only more money in the foot fund, which by month's end was nearly $300, but also the knowledge of knowing where to go. Looking the part of a New Yorker means admitting when you don't know something rather than pretending that you do.

Back at work in September, as I was standing on the corner of Fifth Avenue, a tourist with bags of souvenirs stopped and asked me for directions to Loehmann's. Without hesitation, I laid out the route. "Take Eighteenth Street west to Seventh Avenue and then go two blocks south, it will be on your left, you can't miss it."

September

COFFEE

"Thank you for your coffee, señor.
I shall miss that when we leave Casablanca."
—INGRID BERGMAN, *CASABLANCA*

As I stand in line at 8:00 A.M. on a Wednesday, I noticed that the barista at Starbucks was not moving as quickly as someone whose main job is to refuel a nation. The delay was a result of a high-maintenance order of a tall iced brownie Frappuccino with an extra shot of espresso. Please note: Coffee has rules. Coffee is not to be served with a spoon, topping, or chunks of brownie. Coffee should not be more than 600 calories or have more whipped cream than caffeine. And finally, a morning cup of coffee should not be mistaken for a

Jim Dandy from Friendly's. As orders were shouted and shouted again at the café, I wondered how coffee had gotten so complicated.

Latte, macchiato, and caffè con panna had entered the mainstream vernacular. Keeping pace with this trend led a colleague of mine to an obsession with Starbucks. As quickly as they would build them in Manhattan, when they built them, he would go. The setting of each and every store mesmerized him. He was on a citywide exploration to visit all locations and in doing so, he noted the infinite differences that each location offered. Like a sheikh loves his harem, he usually favored the newest as the best. His taste in Starbucks was much like his taste in women, young and unspoiled. "Have you been to the one on East Fourteenth Street?" he would ask, and "Don't you agree that the one on West Thirty-fifth and Eighth Avenue is far superior to the one just a few blocks away?"

Like my counterparts in the new coffee generation, I demanded much more than a typical cup of joe. As they say on *Law & Order*, motive and opportunity often go hand-in-hand. The same was true for coffee consumption. The plethora of choices made me feel like a kid in a coffee shop. Only this time, I was a spoiled kid who did not know when to quit.

Cards on the table time, my addiction was not only in the morning. Each day, at the conclusion of lunch, I was putty in the hands of anyone who asked the double-edged question "Do you have time for coffee?" Never blessed with a surplus of time, my retaliation was equally cagey. "I do if you do," I volleyed back. The real conversation usually began when facilitated by a strong cup. Passing on the apple pie à la mode was easy, but coffee was a different story. One cup would lead to three as the "coffee enabler" offered to "top that off for you, hon." *Hon* is the secret word that magically coaxes me into drinking three cups in one sitting. I never do that at home.

Escaping from work for a tall steaming cup is a perfectly acceptable corporate ritual. Coffee is the last politically correct vice accepted, and even encouraged, in the workplace. More caffeine means more energy, which means more productivity, which means more work done. Everybody wins on the caffeine hamster wheel. It was inconceivable that so many people drinking coffee could be wrong. This corporate crutch helped us to get up early, work hard, and revive us from the inevitable fatigue from all of the above.

In order to avoid a lunchtime caffeine buzz from

fully fading, a three o'clock coffee break was in order. Some rituals go out of style, but the coffee break is eternal. History shows the coffee break dating back as early as A.D. 1000. Americans began their obsession in the early 1900s, when coffee officially replaced beer as the morning beverage choice. I considered what the office would be like if employees arrived each morning with a six-pack of Guinness to get through each workday. Those were heady times.

The paradoxical purpose of the coffee break is about taking a respite from work while simultaneously getting jacked up on caffeine. After the break, busy bees swing back to the hive with more vitality than before. At least, that is the mantra of the coffee overachiever. At 3:00 P.M., we would go to the nearby City Bakery, which we called "the club" as it had become the favorite coffee hangout for our office. The regular meeting was daily and evolved out of a shared need for the almighty cup. One person would roust from their nest and, like the pied piper leading the children, we would fall into line in a dream state. At times, this movement was performed in silence as we unconsciously began the afternoon crusade. The meeting agenda was expanded to include talking and walking while drinking. Grabbing a cup on the run seemed uncivilized. Soon our coffee break turned into the afternoon "constitutional," using our neighborhood as backdrop for zesty conversation. If done properly, the "constitutional" leaves participants enough time to fully cover office gossip, last night's TV viewings, and which celebrity was annoying us on that given day. At times, the conversations were heated as we vented over ventis. This kind of important information about our social schedules and workday woes could never be discussed over tea. Coffee talk was serious business. Without coffee, this afternoon ritual might not exist.

I resolved to go cold turkey. With all my deep love for coffee, finding a substitute was highly unlikely. The first morning was tough not only for me, but also for my coffee servers. Being the "Norm" of my local coffee shop had its privileges; even the owner knew my daily order. Before uttering the first precoffee words of the day, a glorious piping-hot latte with skim milk would be presented before me.

Part medicinal and part mental, the impetus to get out of bed each morning has always been one simple word and one major addiction, coffee. Without the promise of that first morning cup, my alarm would likely be put on permanent snooze and my thoughts would be contented with endless latte dreams. The anticipation of the first sip propelled a spirited walk to my favorite coffee shop, where it would take every fiber of my noncaffeinated body to resist my Kryptonite: freshly baked raspberry scones. Consolation was found in a less caloric substitute, the morning brew. Coffee was my fail-safe, my rock. Back at the coffee shop on day one, my fail-safe failed me. After I refused the already prepared latte that sat in front of me, an awkward silence ensued. Grappling for something to say, I ordered an unsuspecting raspberry scone instead. What can I say? I panicked.

Not one to jump into a new thing willy-nilly, I knew that a coffee-free life would not be achieved without pain. Terrible headaches resulted from a sudden halt in the caffeine intake. Caffeine Withdrawal Syndrome is a hotly debated condition that doctors are trying to list as an official malady. Even in its unofficial status, my head was beginning to feel like the clapper in the Notre Dame bell. After ingesting several extra glasses of water that day, by three o'clock the intense ache was causing even my eyelashes to hurt. The bell was tolling for me.

That first afternoon, tea offered a solution. How could all those Londoners be wrong? Hearing that it had as much if not more caffeine than coffee, Earl Grey was administered mainly for pain relief. When at the club, I was handed a cup of hot water and asked to pick a tea bag, any tea bag, I began to wonder how a store could actually charge $3.00 for hot water. The idea of traveling with a stash of tea bags in my pocketbook like a favorite granny suddenly had merit. The piping-hot water was presented in all its plainness as I was directed to the beverage condiment bar, where the beverage could be doctored up. Half-and-half, honey, and cinnamon made no improvement to the hollow tastelessness of tea. The once piping-hot beverage was instantly tepid and rendered undrinkable after a series of newfound additives made it lumpy.

Growing up watching older family members prepare their coffee helped form my opinions of them. The creamer and the sugar bowl were like a Rorschach inkblot indicating their deeper selves. As my aunt spooned in three spoonfuls of sugar and not much milk, my uncle did just the opposite, lots of milk with no sugar at all. That taste differential revealed a lot about a couple that managed to disagree about just about everything, but stayed together for nearly forty years. This magic elixir unified even the most disparate personalities.

Days two, three, and four without coffee continued with nagging headache pain, tepid tea drinking, and a lot of Advil. Mentally, there was no consistency. My moods were making sudden turns among intolerance, sudden euphoria, and even paranoia.

It seemed as if everyone else was conducting life inside or outside a Starbucks. The coffee shop was a microcosm. The omnipresence of the coffee bars made them an easy target for meeting friends, killing time between meeting friends, and also, but less likely, meeting for actual coffee. "Let's do lunch," had been replaced by, "Let's grab a cup of coffee." These friendly shops were open layouts encouraging public good behavior. A friend who favors speed dating chooses Starbucks for her initial dates. This new invite was less committed than its precursor, the bar, and less taboo than meeting for a cocktail. The coffee bar was all things to many people. For me all these additional "meetings" jacked the coffee habit up to three and sometimes four cups a day. Despite popular wisdom, if you lead a horse to water, you can make them drink.

Make no mistake, the operative word in coffee shop is coffee. Unable to take part in this societal trend put me on constant alert. Coffeehouses mocked me from every corner. "Why not grab a latte why you wait? You know you want it." My caffeine-free mind saw more and more shops with more and more people drinking out of more and more steaming coffee cups. There was no safe place away from coffee. Even my Pilates classmates were rotating sips of coffee in between core-strengthening exercises.

On week two, searching for substitutes, I tried green tea. For some reason, this tea is always delicious at the sushi restaurant when eating a big bowl of barbecued eel. As a stand-alone substitute for coffee, there was no competition. Green tea tasted like liquid grass. Even after my friend told me about the latest diet trend, which involved eliminating coffee and adding one cup of green tea in its place, did not convert me. This diet promised to have you ten pounds thinner in ten weeks. Apparently green tea is an antioxidant that prevents fat cells in the body. The regimen bans coffee for six months, allowing the antioxidants to take hold in the system. In my caffeine-free zone, it was all I could do not to take hold of my unsuspecting friend's neck. Deprivation does not appreciate unsolicited advice. By the end of the week, I was feeling chock-full of nuts.

The biggest coffee challenge came on a blustery fall

morning upon meeting friends for brunch at my favorite coffee place in the world. And by the world, I mean this place beats the Café Au Lait in Paris and the Café Americano in Italy, and the Costa Rican blend that was delivered to me after a friend traveled to that country last year. The Mac daddy is Cuban coffee, or café con leche, served at La Isla in Hoboken, the best Cuban restaurant in the tri-state area. There they use Café Bustelo, a fine grain of dark coffee that when used at home in a regular percolator creates a consistency much like wet sand. In the capable hands of the café owners, this blend with frothy thick milk is the richest, warmest cup available. Because coffee is my gateway drug, other replacements were tried throughout the entire meal. My consolation drink for that brunch was a papaya mango smoothie.

All these substitutions were taking their toll on my waistline, when at the end of week three I had gained four pounds. The green tea diet might have worked if morning coffee was not replaced at first with raspberry scones and, later, cinnamon buns. While I was in this dejected state, sugar became my latest vice. The afternoon was particularly dangerous, when a chocolate devil's-food cookie became a daily treat.

Even my old standby Dunkin' Donuts was joining

the coffee renaissance. This store was often a no-fly zone, as I could make a half-dozen glazed doughnuts disappear into seemingly thin air. Another branch opened in town, bringing the total to three locations within one square mile. Getting hip to the trend, Dunkin' Donuts added cinnamon lattes and cappuccinos to their menu. These drinks looked pretty, with decorative caramel swirling artfully on top of steaming creamy milk. Under the lid of that tempting cup was nearly 600 caffeinated calories. With those kinds of numbers, why not go with the glazed delights?

Not unlike the bottomless cup at the International House of Pancakes, my love for coffee had no end. Now hitting rock bottom, the buzz began to wear off. A helpful friend recommended Diet Coke in place of coffee. She explained her habits: two cans in the morning, one at lunch with a squeeze of lemon and one as an afternoon break. She was living in a parallel Diet Coke universe. The way she explained her love of Diet Coke was eerily familiar. She, like me, believed the first serving held the secret to happiness. Acknowledging our similar addiction, we came to a meeting of the minds and decided always to carry a bottle of water with us to help replace our caffeinated beverages. Eventually, she kicked the cans down from three to one per day, a palatable solution. With a little help from my friends, habits were being broken and replaced with healthier ones.

I now realized that my need to keep up with the coffee Joneses quickly turned need into a caffeine addiction. Taking a step back this month helped me get the addictive qualities of my coffee drinking in check. Since I never thought of my personality as an addictive one, it was time to reassess what kind of future coffee drinker I would be.

To help sort matters out, I considered all the things that coffee was. Coffee can be ordered with a seven-word description. Coffee is best with biscotti at my local Italian pizzeria. Coffee can be served by a uniformed waitress at a Jersey diner who calls me "hon." Coffee is preferably a steaming cup of café con leche made to perfection at my neighborhood Cuban restaurant. Coffee can be drunk to excess, like Voltaire did in a café named after him in Paris. Coffee fits all of the above and more.

On October 1, I leaped out of bed and headed straight for the coffee shop much like a kid on Christmas morning. Coffee drinking is back in my life, but is now enjoyed in moderation. Drinking four cups every day is a thing of the past. Stepping away from the coffee revolution helped me recognize how much coffee was appropriate to be drinking. Down to one cup in the morning and an occasional afternoon cup, this reduced amount of coffee still manages to satisfy me and knocks the chocolate cookie out of favor. Things seem to be back to normal.

A month of tea drinking has made a new fan of flavored teas. Finally accustomed to green tea, I now drink it almost every day. Old and new habits had now combined, resulting in variety and moderation. And while October taught me to be more cognizant of my habits, the month brought me back in touch with things I already knew but lost appreciation for. Getting up each morning and relishing that first cup is a ritual that will never go away. Cup number one is the best cup of the day, the one that I will continue to look forward to the most. Being a beverage experimentalist was an interesting exercise, but I remain doubtful that my next order at Starbucks will be a brownie Frappuccino.

October

CURSING
F@#%!

> *Words are, of course,*
> *the most powerful drug used by mankind.*
> —RUDYARD KIPLING

I was on the way to JFK airport while dropping off an overseas friend for home, when I asked her what she would miss most about her friends in New York. She replied with a series of colorful expletives that politeness forbids me from recounting word for word. Put more delicately, she admitted that she would miss our permissive language. Surrounded by her potty-mouthed friends, she extolled the positive virtues of our free speech, acclaiming that nobody swears like the New Yorkers! Having spent a good deal of time with this person over the last few weeks, my habits must have been included in her assessment. Celebrating the old saying that variety is the spice of life, I thought my language choices were always appropriate to each situation. At times they could be as dirty as my martinis, but always appropriate, or so I thought.

With my friend's thinly veiled compliment still ringing in my ears, I vowed to clean up my act or at least my mouth. I needed to take inventory of my everyday language.

The originator of the cursing ban came from a business colleague who used curse words as verbs, nouns, adjectives, and adverbs; her swearing had no grammatical rules. Her boss, who had heard enough, would reprimand her daily to "Stop with the language already." He began to penalize her cursing by charging a quarter per infraction. Certainly, if this self-admitted potty mouth could take the challenge, so could I. Together we might move from R to PG 13. It was time to put my money where my mouth was. For this month, bad words were charged a premium of $1.00 each.

With a monetary challenge in place, this month was not only about giving up, but also about giving back. After careful consideration, I elected UNICEF to receive the money collected for infractions. Paying for mistakes would literally create a new awareness for choosing words more carefully. And at least someone would benefit from all this effort. Money would be deposited for each infraction into a curse jar on my desk, serving the dual purpose of bank and visual reminder.

On the first morning's commute, when I just missed the bus by a few seconds, the urge to let loose nearly won out. Instead of letting out a cleansing expletive, my response was to stamp my feet and clench my fist in an act reminiscent of playground antics. Instantly, the adult was replaced by a child. Realizing that this mature demeanor was not something I could maintain on my own, I assigned family, friends, and co-workers as surrogate parents. Like parents, they became the cursing police.

The first day of near misses included closing my finger in the desk drawer, "Oh fudge," and then lunch hour, when the burrito line wrapped around the corner—"Drat," I weakly exclaimed. The day was rife with opportunities to lose control. For the first time, I was conscious that my automatic reaction to these trivial events was usually with an unsavory comment. Particularly alarming was that there was no need for an audience for the outbursts. Let the evidence show an X-rated blabbermouth that appeared to be more schizophrenic than impatient. Biting my tongue reinforced yet another childhood lesson, silence is golden.

Watching my language was setting up a valid argument for not talking at all. It was not that the swearing was so pervasive, it was the reactive impulse of it that concerned me. There is a Joni Mitchell song that captures this feeling, its lyric: "You don't know what you've got till it's gone." Removing the option to swear caused me to slow my speech and think out each word before speaking. Thinking before speaking should not have represented such a revolutionary concept. Most people practice this every day. The time lapse between head and mouth was delaying the rocket-fast retorts that had become my hallmark. I compared it to Dick Van Dyke tripping over the ottoman at the opening of each show. He knows it is there, but he cannot avoid it. This became true of the verbal tripping that had already begun in my mind.

To my credit, the first few days were completed without incident. Awareness was always at hand. In an effort to expand my vocabulary, I subscribed to www.wordsmith.org for help. Each day wordsmith would send a new unfamiliar word to round out my vocabulary that I immediately applied, to the annoyance of those around me. In the future, I would vet other words against wordsmith as not to thwart my clean language process. If for nothing else, a word a day would be a reminder of the ban if not to help find cleaner substitutes.

Following this small success, hopping into my car for an afternoon at the mall should have presented no challenge. Like a petri dish harboring germs, so does the Garden State Parkway bring out the ills of mankind. I was in the driver's seat literally, if not figuratively. Driving in New Jersey requires a certain amount of restraint to begin with; merging onto a highway, pulling out of a gas station, and waiting for a parking spot are all activities that will test your patience. Getting along with not so courteous fellow drivers inevitably results in drivers waving their hands and mouths in mime like gesturing. In soundproof cars, drivers are free to rattle off every swearword in the book.

Spying a great parking space at the mall, I began to signal left. A car suddenly appeared and cut me off, heading right at the space. That meanie did not even signal. Honking the horn and screaming expletives into the closed window of my Honda, I sped forward to claim the space. The good news was that the space was mine. The bad news was that my blood pressure was raised to unhealthy proportions. The curse jar had its first deposit with a conservative $6.00. This break-down reminded me of watching pro sports, where even though the sound is muted, Shaquille O'Neal can be seen mouthing off after taking a hard foul against the Pistons. In the parking garage that day, Shaq and I had much in common.

Avoiding cursing enabled me to realize that the entire world was airing its dirty laundry and dirty mouths around me. Walking through the neighborhood during the first week, my ears would perk up every time an infraction was heard. A good example comes from my own backyard, which is located near a middle school. I was taking a sick day, and was propped bliss-fully on my couch. *General Hospital* had just begun. As the familiar ambulance rolled into the driveway at the show's beginning, I hunkered down for an afternoon of eagerly awaited soap opera watching. Suddenly, as heard through my window, four-letter words being bandied about like beads during Mardi Gras. Outside, five middle school boys were screaming as many curse words as they could as loudly as they could. School was out indeed. There was no safe haven from swearing. That was day ten and the urge to crane my neck out the window and answer in kind was nearly overwhelming. Telling the boys to watch their language and then calling them "poo poo heads" just did not pack the same punch.

Equipped with an internal alarm for early detection caused the curse itself to be redefined. Like a party guest that does not get the hint, curses had staked their territory for the long haul. The once taboo words were now common usage, reinforced on cable television, in the movies, at the office, even on the street corner, making them acceptable. If the advice of my catechism nun were to be taken, the word "Jeez" was also a curse. Using this word in vain will land you at the head of the confession line. This month, I banned commonly used profane words, including "Jeez," as a special courtesy to Sister Lorraine. The addition of that rule cost two more dollars and an instant trip to confession. For clarity's sake, the standard swearwords that George Carlin rattles off so eloquently in his ten-second dialogue are the standard-bearer.

As the second week began, I searched for the right substitute words to express my frustration. Using a curse when more descriptive words were available in my lexicon was a cop-out. Call it laziness, habit, or just bad form, a swearword was an easier, if not more expressive choice. Most, if not all, of these choices were being made unconsciously. An informal poll of friends and family indicated that my language was more suited for HBO than for PAX. What people said was surprising, my sterling reputation needed polishing.

Growing up with three older brothers included playing games such as "Mailbox." Mailbox involved sending letters between my room and my brothers' rooms in an ongoing correspondence that mimicked the real postal service. This glorified way of passing notes featured crude drawings of stamps and postage marks, a faux under-the-door mail slot, and instant delivery.

After several mail deliveries, we got creative. At twelve, my brother pushed the envelope by sending an offer for a subscription to *Playboy* magazine. Never wanting to be topped by the older boys, the return mail included an article that might have appeared in the magazine. The first issue was intercepted by our mother, who quickly learned that her eight-year-old daughter not only had a working knowledge of anatomy, but an ability to write colorful descriptions to guide the reader. That discovery marked the official end to Mailbox punctuated with a mouthful of Ivory soap. This experience awakened an interest in writing as a favored form of expression.

Fumbling for the words at the beginning of this October brought back those flavorful soap-filled memories. Once again, the time had come for crime and punishment. What differed in adulthood was that there was no parent to keep me in line. Left to my own devices, there would only be willpower and concentration to rely on. With all that was going on in my busy life, it was difficult to remember to pay attention to these small language details.

Admitting this vice to co-workers and friends was uncomfortable. Would they think less of me for having to give up such a bad habit? Admitting that there was a need to limit cursing highlighted the abuse, something tough to come to terms with. After revealing my plan to my office, not only did they not think less of me, they were doubtful that anyone could do it. One co-worker confirmed that he would be unable to get through the daily commute without sounding off in one way or another. The goal of this month was not to stifle all emotions and ignore life's daily injustices, but to react to them differently, without forked tongue.

Another co-worker explained her biggest temptation would be to deposit $10.00 in the till at the beginning of the day and then swear her head off. She had a point. Instead, the curse jar would cause a loud cling in the glass jar, taking all mystery out of the progress report. This was made more obvious by the first installment from the mall incident as twenty-four quarters were loudly deposited.

My office environment like many others was relaxed, resembling a college dormitory more than a business environment. We were friends with little need for formality and our language reflected that. Extra hours, entertaining, and work outings contributed to a more laid-back atmosphere. Even the dress code had loosened up in line with a more casual lifestyle. While not suggesting that my language was better when back in the 1990s when I was wearing a Brooks Brothers suit rather than Levi jeans and a turtleneck, my modern-day office was more laid back in every way. Certainly, the atmosphere promoted more freedom in all things, speech included.

The idea of freedom of speech when discussing swearing is an important lesson. My college journalism program was taught by an interesting and expressive group of writers. While the childhood classroom represented restraint and discipline, the college classroom emphasized experimentation and, for many fellow students, a newfound freedom. The college editing professor embodied this philosophy. His class introduction might have been more suitable for an episode of *The Sopranos* than a classroom. He used a full array of four-letter words, some of which were new to me. This teacher could give George Carlin a run for his money.

Although I was shocked by the language within the classroom, his boldness had an instant effect on me and my fellow classmates. We were impressed by his rebellious style and confidence and immediately dubbed him the superlative "cool." Ironically, while teaching the rules of line editing, it became clear that he might be in need of an editor of his own. The editorial marking of "WC," or word choice, was only one of the lessons that were taught in this class and had an ironic twist in this case. "WC" was used when a better word can be replaced to make a sentence clearer. The teacher would likely argue that many of the expletives he used with loving familiarity had no substitutes.

Finding no substitute was my downfall as the second week came to a close. A friend announced her engagement and was greeted with some choice words other than congratulations. Two dollars proved that bad words can be appropriate for good occasions, bringing the balance to $8.00. It was impossible to let my guard down without paying the consequences.

As the month continued, everyone's speech habits had become magnified. While at a bistro, a woman at the next table opted to break up with her boyfriend on the cell phone as he had kept her waiting through the appetizer and half a bottle of Pinot Noir. He was not *bleeping* where he was supposed to be last night and tonight was *bleeping* late as well. This conversation became much more emphatic with her colorful adjectives. Excuse her French!

Words had a will of their own. This became apparent on a weekend getaway with friends during the end of the second week of cursing abstinence. Unfortunately, a rainstorm kept us from a bike ride and we opted for Scrabble instead. Always a competent player, I was excited to take part. Only this time it was Scrabble with a twist, requiring the use of slang and naughty words. Finishing dead last was not an option for the competitor in me. I scrabbled my way to a $10.00 infraction. Unfortunately, this deposit did not help to win the game. The third week showed a total of $20.00 in the curse account. This was a lot of money for someone who thought that her language was suitable enough to be used in front of her grandmother. For the rest of the month, I would try to envision her in the room before opening my mouth.

With the devil ahead in the contest, I became more committed during the final week of the month. Sensitivity was heightened. Later that week, our book group was meeting to discuss the month's selection, *Peter Pan*. Each member took a turn to give a perspective on the book's theme, topics, and what they found to be the most surprising aspects of the story. In the book, Tinkerbell is portrayed as a character that is not as nice as Disney led us to believe. The original Tink was a vindictive potty mouth who often could not be directly quoted in mixed company. Most of her time was spent flouncing around taunting Peter Pan. The group was taken aback by the image of this childhood icon, now tarnished. We marveled that this image associated with good and sweet was not as she appeared. It was comforting to know that I was not the only one needing a Disney makeover.

As the month came to a close, I found myself waiting in line at a local movie theater; my fellow line mates were an elderly couple and two teenage girls. The teenage girls were talking to each other loudly in order to be heard over their blasting iPods. The elderly couple and I quickly noticed the language that the girls were using, not once, not twice, but three times. As we made our way to the front of the line and out of earshot of the two girls, the older man turned and we exchanged a head shake. Suddenly, I had become one of the parents on the line, mentally finger pointing at "kids today."

With that formative lesson, I came to realize that swearing had begun in my youth and had never been corrected in adulthood. Societal influences condone bad language and the only steps to changing that behavior is through effort, concentration, and a little help from those around you. The addition of the monetary penalty, the curse jar, did little as a deterrent. Like any career criminal will tell you, consequence is not considered when acting in the heat of passion. Swearing was an act of passion that unconsciously had become part of my everyday speech. The final tally for the jar was $20.00, which when matched with my own contribution resulted in a $40.00 contribution to my charity of choice, UNICEF. I chose UNICEF because of its excellent work with children, and since this month in essence taught me about my inner child, the choice seemed fitting.

The journey had come full circle. I am now more aware of language and the role it plays. What was most interesting was the role that I played in the context of different situations. It remained to be seen if the parent or the child would emerge. What exists now that did not exist before the month began is the basic notion of thinking before speaking, which should be an automatic adult response. For me, this was managed with difficulty, and it is a lesson that I carry with me every day. The way I communicate has changed as a result. Eliminating cursing 100 percent from my vocabulary is not all that likely, especially if I plan ever to drive my car again. But being more conscious of it makes it easier to eliminate some of the occurrences. My search for the right words has only just begun.

November

CHOCOLATE

The average American consumes
11.64 lbs. of chocolate per year.
—*THE ATLAS OF CHOCOLATE*

Chocolate holds the top spot on my all-time list of favorite things. This fact was documented during a parlor game entitled "What Would You Rather?" This game, spun off by the once popular, but recently tired, game of "Who Would You Rather," forced a choice between two Hollywood heartthrobs and an invitation to "spend the evening." After weighing the merits of countless celebrities who would never be met in countless scenarios that would never happen, we began to get a bit craftier. After all, choosing between George

Clooney and Brad Pitt was by all counts a no-lose situation. Accounting for personal tastes and trends, the heartthrob du jour could be interchanged to effect the same outcome. Human nature was determined when real choices became part of the game, giving birth to an odd hybrid version. On one memorable occasion, Harrison Ford was pitted against Buffalo wings. My choice would leave Harrison to spend the night alone, because a spicy, crispy bucket of wings were keeping me warm at night.

The game was played much like a pro tennis match until finally the player would be volleying back the same answer over and over and over again. The straw that broke the camel's back came with the choice between Buffalo wings and chocolate, creating a cruel *Sophie's Choice*–like moment. Brad Pitt, George Clooney, Harrison Ford, and Steven Tyler had lost in early rounds to one another and then to various food items, until finally I exclaimed repeatedly, chocolate, chocolate, and chocolate! With this knowledge and a leftover Halloween bag of Hershey's miniatures, I embraced the deep dark obsession.

October 31 was a windfall for the chocolate lover. This holiday not only condoned, but also encouraged the inner chocolate junkie in me. Throughout the years, my brothers and I would don ridiculous costumes, grab king-sized pillowcases, and storm the neighborhood, demanding that our chocolate addiction be fed. Like many things in my childhood, competition sat firmly at the center of this activity, pitting sibling against sibling in a race to get the most candy. After all the kids returned home, my mother would conduct a search-and-seizure of the pillowcases, indicating which one of us had the most and also what we would be able to keep. Growing up in suburban New Jersey during the 70s and 80s, there was suspicion that the razor-blade apple or LSD laced-Razzle package could be lurking in any of our trick-or-treat bags. Overprotective parents like mine had to be careful about the reckless disregard for courtesy and decorum that this holiday represented. Halloween not only allowed for it, but encouraged going to strangers' homes and demanding things. If only that holiday carried over to other parts of life.

One by one, we were told to drop 'em (our bag, that is) while the candy was fanned out on the kitchen table. Like a diamond appraiser with a loupe, my mother held each piece up to the light to determine if the candy was safe enough to eat. She would then make piles for each: throw out, good enough for the kids and finally "Dad's bag." "Dad's bag" was the receptacle for all the iffy chocolate bars and candy necklaces that were determined not fit for kids but most likely not laced with anything that would harm my father. Always a culinary risk taker, Dad welcomed the challenge these irregular candy pieces offered. In his words, this candy "had nothing wrong with it." Like our own Rasputin, he defiantly ate BB Bats, Bit-O-Honeys, and Mary Janes, throwing caution to the wind.

The bag itself was a rumpled-up brown paper one possessing a questionable look on its own, but when coupled with weird Zagnut bars and smashed-up Smarties, "Dad's bag" was downright scary. The bag's home was in a lower kitchen cabinet alongside little-used canned goods and unpopular baking ingredients. The bag would remain there through Christmas and the New Year. One year, the bag lasted all the way to Easter, but fell short of our secret wish of a one-year anniversary. Dad had made his way through his bag by then. As our trick-or-treating days came to an end, my musical family had even perfected a theme song to accompany each candy on its journey to "Dad's bag." To this day, any family members will recall the familiar song whose lyrics can be sung to the melody of the *Munsters'* opening scenes.

The house favorite was the Snickers bar, combining an unprecedented nougat, caramel, peanuts, and chocolate. At 5 Berry Hill Court, in the week that followed Halloween, trading treats was all the rage and chocolate was a hot commodity.

Once in a blue moon, I would trade my all-time favorite, the Chunky bar, raisins and nuts in a solid cube of chocolate enrobed in silver paper. Recipients of this bar could easily have the pick of the litter from my stash. I even created a special way of eating this candy to prolong our time together. The Chunky bar would be systematically eaten block by block, forming perfect cubelike bites along the way.

These formative lessons in chocolate instilled a lifetime respect for the confection. Recalling these stories on November 1, led me to review an adult habit that had ranged from two to four pieces daily. More often than not, one piece would lead to another and before I knew it, an entire bag of Goobers would be gone faster than you can say obsessive-compulsive.

Tastes had been refined over the years, at times preferring a piece of chocolate to the actual chocolate bar, which now seemed piggish. Pound for pound, I would probably eat less chocolate if I were to eat the entire Twix bar than if a bag of Hershey's Kisses were opened in front of me. Polishing off an entire bag of chocolate seemed less offensive when eating bite-size pieces over the course of an afternoon. If I were left alone with a started bag of chocolate, a clean-plate philosophy was sure to ensue.

At the time, Lindt chocolate truffles from Switzerland were my current favorite. They came in several flavors and were conveniently sold individually wrapped at most delis and lunch spots. Since I was always a cash-register impulse shopper, it was hard to resist grabbing that little ball of chocolate to accompany the vegan asparagus salad chopped into minuscule pieces. A girl had to have some fun. Dietary trading always included chocolate as the prize. The Halloween years and a good poker game supported the *Let's Make a Deal* diet that was part of life.

No matter how big or small the serving was, chocolate to me was necessary on a daily basis. After lunch and dinner, a chocolate kiss or a small cookie would cap off the meal. Like my addiction to coffee, chocolate perked me up and immediately made me happy. Scientific research backs this up as well. Dark chocolate has been noted as having properties that release a chemical in the brain that causes euphoria. Living without the happy bar was not something I looked forward to, believing in my heart that just a little bit here and there couldn't be too bad. What I came to realize was that many times, once the chocolate eating had begun, there was no turning back.

November with its fall scents and flavors was a natural time to go choco free; many autumnal substitutes could be sampled. Reasoning that the chocolate was a sugar addiction, the diagnosis was rendered. Sugar could be found in other treats such as a lemon cookie or an apple dumpling, both delicious, and could even be given points for including fruit. Skipping chocolate temporarily should have been no problem with so many other cocoa-free substitute treats waiting to take its place.

The first order of business would be to rid the house of all chocolate temptation. Ghirardelli hot chocolate mix, Bosco, Chipwiches, and even Baker's bittersweet chocolate were given away. The leftover windfall from Halloween was reluctantly distributed at work. A big bowl of chocolate lasted only till two o'clock on the first day, indicating the confection's popularity among my colleagues as well as myself. One co-worker was caught red-handed eating a mini-Krackel bar at 10:30 A.M., claiming that she had skipped coffee that morning and needed a little pick-me-up. Chocolate was appropriate at any hour.

Once the chocolate was removed from my physical space, the true battle against the internal chocolate demons began. The decision to make chocolate off limits caused an immediate craving. Could it be possible that this chocolate temptation always existed? Was the Godiva chocolates store always two blocks from my home? It seemed nowhere was safe. Checking out at the bookstore even posed a problem. A dark chocolate raspberry bar seemed to sprout legs and plead to accompany the new Bridget Jones novel home with me. And that was only week one.

After making a concerted effort to avoid all chocolate, a routine food shopping only aggravated my condition. The candy aisle of my local ShopRite presented more temptations than the Garden of Eden. Boldly walking down that aisle brought back all the sentimental memories of my chocolate-coated youth. Each candy had something to say: "You got chocolate on my peanut butter," shouted the Reese's peanut butter cups over the drone of the "Sometimes you feel like a nut," melody of the Almond Joy. The M&Ms told me they melted in my mouth not in my hands, which provided little comfort. Even the York peppermint patties whetted my appetite, which is very odd as they have never been my favorites. I never believed the ad campaign showing a housewife-turned-champion-skier extolling the candy's cool sensation. On the other side of the aisle, Mrs. Fields was weighing in, with Archway and Stella D'oro close behind. I increased my pace and planned to avoid the baked goods area at all costs. All of them included chocolate and were also off limits. Yodels, Ring Dings, and Big Wheels, oh my!

By the beginning of week two, solutions were harder to come by. When I turned on the television with a bag of yogurt-covered raisins in hand, the announcer taunted, "Do you dream in chocolate?" He never said, "Do you dream in carob?" or "Do you dream in yogurt?" There was a reason for that; neither of those substitutes tastes as good as chocolate. It was simply better.

My uncle Richard, a lifelong motorcycle rider, tells a story that applies to this situation. He explains that many first-time riders will unintentionally ride directly into whatever is in front of them, hitting poles and fences instead of swerving to miss them. This was also true for chocolate addicts. Once the attention is fixed on chocolate, avoiding it becomes nearly impossible.

A night at the movies was reinforcement. Always a creature of habit, my first stop at the Cineplex was always the snack bar, where sweet, salty, and sour mix to create the perfect all-around snack. After successfully avoiding the 8:00 P.M. showing of *Chocolat,* which would have been cruel and unusual punishment, the biggest challenge lay straight ahead, the snack bar. Like the *Titanic* heading for the iceberg, danger could not be averted. Placing the regular order of Sour Patch Kids, small popcorn no topping, and Diet Coke, I hesitated. The next step would include a trip to the candy bar, where Whoppers, bridge mix, and Sno-Caps would be shoveled into a paper bag. This smorgasbord of candy bins afforded the noncommittal snacker a little bit of everything. While I hesitated over the Rolos, the cashier taunted me by asking, "Will there be anything else?" Usually a victim of this kind of cinematic hard selling, I would cave and fill the bag with $12.00 in weighty treats. With hands firmly on the wheel, the *Titanic* turned course as I offered an emphatic "no." This time, no actually meant no. This stick-to-my-guns attitude helped to squelch the craving. At the very least, saying it, if not believing it, would help to sidestep temptations.

Wanting things you cannot have is a classic human condition. The experience at the movie theater helped deliver a newfound white-knuckle approach.

At my desk that next Monday morning, lunch was laid out before me. Veggie chili and pita accompanied by a cantaloupe with pretzel rods for an afternoon snack. My mind leaped to the inadequacy of this snack. Dipping pretzels into Nutella would have created a chocolate hazelnut treat. Nearly every food could have been enhanced if coated in chocolate. Substitutes only paled in comparison as the plotting began to thicken. At a Mexican restaurant, would mole sauce count and what about white chocolate? Café mocha? The bargaining distracted the visions of Toll-House cookies that were constantly dancing in my head. There had to be some way to satisfy this craving without breaking my abstinence.

Sampling other treats was initially interesting, but trouble quickly arose when waiters presented my nemesis, the dessert menu. Up until this month, I would not even read the other menu choices. My mantra was always, Why order dessert unless it is chocolate? At dinner during the second week, those around the table responsibly split chocolate fondue and molten chocolate cake while I looked on enviously.

Declining the fondue led to lively discourse and debate. The incredulous audience was awed by the uphill battle of a world without chocolate. Each diner appeared to be an expert. Soon the chocolate sides were drawn. The debate pit: Fauchon against Lindt, Godiva against Dove Bar. One person even extolled the virtues of Hershey's. Everyone had an opinion. There was certainly more to chocolate than just candy.

Left with no other alternative, I adopted the "if you can't beat 'em, join 'em" philosophy. Satisfying the desire for chocolate would be sated with becoming a connoisseur. If not able to eat it, at least I could read about it. Knowing that November was only thirty days and the holidays promised a chocolate lover's paradise, this research project was viewed as good preparation. Secretly, the thought of unpeeling colored foil from a mini-Santa was overwhelming.

As a result of the chocolate-coated dinner, I started a chocolate journal, carefully taking notes of stores and brands that I had yet to try. There was no lack of material for the journal, as everyone around was contributing. Williams-Sonoma was even e-mailing hot chocolate recipes, making me feel as if I were at the center of a chocolate conspiracy.

This became further evident as the holiday baskets for Thanksgiving and Christmas began to arrive in our offices with more and more frequency. A well-intended vendor unwittingly stepped into a land mine when sending me a variety pack of Ghirardelli candy bars. "Who would send such a thing?" I shouted. This reaction was less than thankful, as the basket included every elegantly packaged flavor of chocolate. Bringing these bars to an upcoming meeting made me once again very popular, but increasingly depressed.

The foil packaging was reminiscent of the ultimate chocolate lover's fantasy manual, *Charlie and the Chocolate Factory*. The plot centers around a contest to find the gold wrapper in Wonka chocolate bars. Those who found the gold foil won a trip to the chocolate factory. The lesson was delivered when not only was the chocolate process demystified, but the very nature of humankind was revealed. Much to the ignorance of the contest participants, Mr. Wonka was looking for a substitute for the dream job, a successor to take over his factory. If I were given that opportunity, the profits would surely be eaten.

My thoughts would often wander back to the movie; the factory replete with a chocolate river had taken over my imagination. Getting into a gingerbread gondola and rolling down a bittersweet river seemed a great way to travel. Back in chocolate-free reality, these memories kept me afloat.

Willie Wonka was a worthy role model for the emerging chocolate connoisseur. Learning about chocolate was easy to do with hundreds of Web sites, Food Network programs, radio commentary, and magazine articles all lauding its virtues. There were chocolate clubs and retail sites, books devoted to its preparation and evolution. It was comforting to read the stories of other chocoholics, like the ancient Aztec Montezuma, who was rumored to drink fifty cups of hot chocolate a day. His people, believed to be the creators of chocolate, used it as both currency and aphrodisiac. While the virtues of chocolate as an aphrodisiac remain to be seen, the argument for chocolate as currency was making a case. Having become a chocolate benefactor at work and at home reinforced the idea that with chocolate, some people would do most anything to get it.

As the chocolate quest continued, fellow chocoholics were soon discovered. Katharine Hepburn, one of my all-time favorite actresses, had eaten nearly half a pound a day. In New York City, there was an entire trade show devoted to chocolate. Phoebe, a self-admitted chocoholic, attended the show and was amazed by what she described as the United Nations of chocolate. A puritan of sorts, her mission at the show was to sample and purchase champagne truffles. The difficulty of her search became apparent as none of the hundred or so booths carried the elusive truffle. When asking a dashingly dressed Parisian for insight, Phoebe was met with a guffaw and the dismissal "Truffles are so last year!" Apparently, the world of chocolate has an elite class. Phoebe eventually had to settle for sniffing out truffles at her local mall.

Like Phoebe, I was searching for a specific chocolate experience. When I was a child, this experience began with the Keebler Fudge Stripes cookie. The elves make a full line of chocolate-covered cookies, including my mother's favorite, the Deluxe Grahams; my favorite, the Fudge Stripes; and my brother's favorite, the Fudge Sticks. Each variety starts with a cookie and is then made unique through shape and size. The common denominator is the chocolate covering. Finding one cookie that was different was a fascinating pursuit. The uniformity of the packaging and the exact striping made me pessimistic. It seemed implausible that these cookies were, well, cookie cutter. The quest would begin with the after-school snack consisting of two rows from the package. Once in a while, the quality control would be rewarded by finding two cookies stuck together or a stripe that was not quite straight. When reviewing this habit, it seems more Rain Man than Candy Man.

This month, my chocolate research project was being fed by all I mentioned it to. A friend sent an article that urged support for the medical virtues of chocolate. Preliminary studies linked chocolate to improved cardiovascular health, lower risks for certain types of cancer, and a slowing down of the aging process. Thoughts of living longer while eating pound bags of M&Ms had their appeal. Of course, if it seems too good to be true, it probably is. Further research indicated that not all chocolates are created equal. The linchpin ingredient to the live-long-and-eat-chocolate theory is cocoa flavonol, which varies in amount depending on the manufacturer. Even though my habit was situated on the corner of science and indulgence streets, science would not solely be able to justify my habit.

When looking for reasons why I ate chocolate every

day, the bottom line appeared. I loved chocolate. Living without it was not an option. Finding new ways to eat chocolate was an entertaining way to spend the month, but it was no substitute for eating it. As the month came to a close, the urge to have chocolate was magnified. I went to sleep on November 30 knowing that when waking, a special day was coming.

On December 1, I headed directly to the local café, where instead of one latte, a frothy extra-large hot chocolate was raised in respect to Montezuma. This treat had no whipped cream or marshmallows, no distractions from the full-bodied taste of the cocoa. With my love for chocolate renewed, I sought new ways to extend the enjoyment, even including chocolate toppers on all gifts this year. I had learned that going without something loved is not something I would wish on anyone. Chocolate is best when shared. All of the information that I learned about chocolate led to a listing of my favorites, which I share and discuss with fellow chocolate experts. The list was enjoyed within the first few days of December, proving once again that November was the cruelest of months.

The suitable epilogue to this chocolate strife came as a holiday gift, literally. Living in an older apartment building presents unfixable problems. As December began and the need for heat and hot water became mandatory, mine decided to take an early holiday. After several phone calls and more than a few repairmen, there was still no heat as the holiday season neared. All I wanted for Christmas was to not wear head-to-toe fleece inside. After a holiday dinner with friends in town, I entered my apartment to find a present. On my kitchen table, the landlord had left a box of handmade chocolates. I was overwhelmed by his kindness. The large box included nut clusters, turtles, coconut hay-stacks, and bittersweet nougats. It was a fantastic selec-tion, which was enjoyed immediately. Overwhelmed by this gesture, I decided to be a bit more patient about the heat; after all, it was not his fault that the old building could not be fixed. In the final analysis, when consid-ering what I would rather have, it would have to be chocolate over heat.

December

MULTITASKING

In proportion, as he simplifies his life,
the laws of the universe will appear less complex.
—HENRY DAVID THOREAU, *WALDEN*

Proving once again that man cannot live by bread alone, this month's challenge came with a side of nan bread at a neighborhood Indian restaurant. A novice waitress was having trouble taking our rapid-fire order. Much to our dismay at the time, she spilled a bowl of soup on us and served the couple next to us only cold bread for the first thirty minutes of the meal. Scrambling to clean up and get back to another demanding table, she added the statement that would shape this month's challenge: "Hold on, I can only do one thing at a time."

While doing a bit of scrambling of my own, I began to consider a deeper meaning. Taking her advice literally, I started a personal revolution, "unitasking."

The approaching holiday season demanded getting as much done as possible at any one time, or what is commonly known as "multitasking." Originally, this term was used for computers able to perform more than one task at a time, such as printing out labels while e-mailing your aunt Sally and checking out the latest cable knits on www.jcrew.com. Making the Dell laptop work double time was one thing, but trying to follow suit was taxing my personal operating system. As the month began, I felt mentally handcuffed by my daily "to do" list, unable to make good decisions among the distractions. Like many of my friends, I was stressed out. Instead of succumbing to a restless December with dark circles under my eyes and a fake smile on my face, I decided to take control, by taking back the holidays. In the Wild West property of my mind, there was a new sheriff in town.

When putting together the holiday shopping list, which reached an all-time high of twenty-five recipients, I questioned how everything would get done in one month. The notion of buying one well-thought-out gift for each recipient was clearly not going to be possible. The most wonderful time of the year began to look less than wonderful. That carefree child on Christmas morning had matured into a jaded consumerist, impatiently waiting on line at Macy's in an ill-fated attempt to get a jump on holiday shopping. After a fruitless search for a very specific bathrobe for my father, I settled on a pair of slippers that claimed to have state-of-the-art comfort. These double-duty shoes were like walking on air. When paying and handing over my customer appreciation coupon, my mind hopped to the next shopping topic, which was determining which potato ricer to purchase for my aunt. Shortly after the cell phone rang just as I was signing the receipt, and an awkward juggling of the slippers, sales receipt, and cell phone ensued, resulting in a curt conversation with the Macy's salesperson. The month had not even begun and I already realized how pervasive multitasking was in daily life.

This one gift at a time pace was going to take twenty-four more store trips to aptly reward all the nice people on my list. It stood to reason that purchasing one thing at a time was not going to do the job. Without the assistance of Santa's elves, shopping stress was putting the bah humbug into this favorite time of year. Balancing the pressures of the season with work, workout, and social life would not be easy.

I was pondering the idea of balance when sitting at my office. The basics of my desktop included: laptop, cell phone, office phone, and CD player, all designed to make my life easier. The ever-expanding technology revolution can be overwhelming. With so many choices and upgrades, it is easy to get confused. A phenomenon that is not exclusive to technology. One need only take a trip down the cereal aisle at ShopRite, flip through 100 Direct TV channels, or order a coffee beverage at Starbucks to notice the constant need for decision making.

Falling victim to this trend, I traded up to a personal desk assistant. The handheld device was supposed to be more efficient and far superior to the dinosaur Filofax and pencil set I had toted around for years. The honeymoon ended quickly after several attempts to maneuver the miniature pencil onto the miniature screen, which made me feel like Gulliver. The modern device that was intended to make life easier, required more attention than it was worth. Technology had left me in the dust.

Coupling these attention-seeking devices with the interruptions of the usual workday, visitors, package deliveries, and meetings created a day doomed for distraction. With all of these competing choices, completing one task from start to finish appeared unrealistic. While sitting at my desk, I would check voice mail, sort through papers on my desk, and look over e-mail. The task, regardless of what it was, would be sidetracked as soon as the phone rang. Picking up phones during any situation is now an accepted business practice. During meetings, ring tones would indicate that people were to be available at all times. "Let me take this call," allows workers to opt out of a meeting. As if channel surfing to find a better radio station, everyone seemed to be looking for a better conversation.

Concentrating on one thing at a time was uncharted territory for me. My mind could best be compared to an Oliver Stone movie where multiple ideas bombard the viewer simultaneously, making for good storytelling but little clarity. It seemed that once I put this new idea out in the universe, an answer, no matter how odd it might have seemed at the time, was provided. While I realize that there are no coincidences, the universe answered quickly when I was attending a business networking meeting where I met an energy healer. At first unfamiliar with the notion that my energy, or anyone else's for that matter, needed to be healed, I listened somewhat skeptically to this new information.

After a brief conversation, which covered personal challenges, general health, and goals, the doctor rendered a diagnosis. It should be noted that while this conversation ensued, my mind was wandering from what outfit would be worn to dinner that night to what my next meal would consist of to whether or not the dry cleaner was still open to pick up the gray skirt. Focusing back and feeling a bit like I was being diagnosed, sarcasm got the better of me. A fantasy conversation played out in my mind where I told the doctor that "it hurts when I multitask," to bait her into saying, "Stop multitasking."

Noticing that my scrambled energy needed a closer look, the energy healer handed over an appointment card for later that week. This appeared to be a wise course of action, but ironically it added another task to an already jam-packed week. That time might have been better spent staring at the walls in a Zenlike state than hustling onto the subway to attain the elixir. Considering this month to be about self-improvement, pushing out of the comfort zone might provide some help. With deep-seated skepticism about success rate, I clutched onto the olive branch.

At the appointment, where a cabinet full of oils were suggestively sold, I answered a series of unrelated questions, including diet, workout, marital status, and favorite television show. After answering, healthy diet, frequent yoga, happy relationship, and *Law & Order,* I had the tools for serenity in hand. Among the oils was one aptly named Present Time, which when applied to the third chakra should be accompanied by a simple chant, "Let me live in the moment."

The next day before work, I applied the oils with coordinating chants. In addition, Brain Power, a particularly distasteful oil, was applied to the tongue, which caused me to do two things at one time, chant and retch.

When I was answering e-mail, the phone rang. Instead of cradling the phone on my shoulder while typing away responses, I stopped, dumbfounded about what to do. Echoes of "Live in the moment" ricocheted through my mind. Answering the call was the priority for that moment. With that decided, the call was answered and completed, and then e-mail correspondence was resumed. While the act was not hard, the mental energy to retrain these involuntary steps was exhausting. At 9:05, it was far too early to do any back patting. The morning continued the same way, the phone rang, the e-mail poured in, office mates stopped by, and the schedule became fuller and fuller. All the while, holiday sales, Christmas cards, and baking cookies danced in my head. With twenty-four more gifts to buy, would it be bad form to shop on www.bananarepublic. com while on a conference call? These temptations indicated a need for focus.

Until this month, my thoughts would come quickly, randomly, and without respect for one another, not dissimilar to rush hour traffic at the Holland Tunnel. At the mouth of the tunnel, a police officer directs traffic.

Perhaps a traffic cop would have to monitor the traffic in my mind. My "to do" list would creep up the outside lanes of doing laundry and making dinner, meetings at work would rudely cut off all others. My mental freeway was gridlocked until I consciously made the decision to take control.

Whenever check-in is required at hotels, parties, or events, the need for focus and listening skills becomes apparent. With a last name like Carlomagno, there is always variety in spellings and pronunciation. When checking in, my line usually goes, first name Mary and last name begins with C, as I spell out C-A-R. Without fail, the person at the desk begins leafing through the letter M, asking, What is the spelling? M? A? G? As I try to direct the person back to the letter *C,* a small "aha" moment occurs when the realization that he or she did not focus on what was said hits. Not listening is a direct result of multitasking. Taking time to listen to what another is saying requires focus and precious time, both of which is in short supply.

Time is a luxury and doing one thing at a time does not keep pace with our busy lifestyles, which demand doing more. But if we do more, more inefficiently, what has really been accomplished? In the office, while working at our desk, a call comes in and we neglect the work at hand, our boss comes in to schedule a meeting while a client demands last-minute reports. One morning when I was juggling office tasks, a colleague stopped by to tell of a change in meeting place. Preoccupied with something else, I did not take the time to listen to what was said. Even though I nodded agreement, I did not pay attention and showed up at the wrong conference room.

The need to slow down and focus was reinforced on the mat as Jake, my yoga teacher, intervened. He asks his students at the beginning of each class to take a moment to forget about whatever happened before the class and to forget what needs to be done after the class. He urges us to let go of the guy that cut us off on the road on the way to class or the negative phone call placed to the landlord earlier that morning. This is easier said by him than done by me. His point is to enjoy the place you are now, in effect to get out of your own way. This Eastern thinking switches the emphasis and minimizes a tendency to save up for later. That rainy day was now.

As an organized person who tends to plan more for the rainy day than the present sunny day, my daily planner is the bible for all activity. When a task is completed, it is crossed off the page, after a workout a gold star is applied, meetings and lunches are scheduled weeks in advance, and all is systematically planned away. Hitting these arbitrary dates and times like an actor hitting his mark was not a quality way to live. This frenzied pace has caused people to consider a different way.

In the 1980s a cultural antimovement evolved out of a need for less materialistic living. This movement, called Voluntary Simplicity, is seeing resurgence as Web sites and publications extol the simpler life. This lifestyle advocates eliminating material distractions, cutting spending and consumerism, and in essence retreating to simpler times. Thoreau's modern counterparts seek a simpler life through drastic life change. And while leaving corporate trappings behind is extremely seductive to my circle of friends, we have other ways to get us through the workday.

In England and Australia, people are spending less time on fantasizing and are creating their own escape routes. High-paced executives are opting out of their high-paced executive lives and choosing voluntarily to downshift. This term adopted from a car downshifting its gears means to slow the pace of life to allow a healthier existence. In his book, *Hotel Pastis,* Peter Mayle illustrates this beautifully when a hotshot advertising partner ultimately chooses the simpler life of hotel owner in the south of France over his million-dollar corporate life. There is tremendous appeal for doing less to become more fulfilled.

While my colleagues and I tick dates off our Franklin Planners, it seems an unconscious countdown is on. Each item ticked off will get us closer to our goal, vacation, finishing a big project, and finally year end. By midmonth, I hated the daily planner as it doubled as a minefield where hitting social marks was taking precedent over all else.

My colleague often overschedules himself and approaches his calendar every Monday and frantically downshifts the entire week. He is always surprised at the number of commitments he has marked down and his inability to carry through with them. Many times, my Filofax listed multiple engagements which required that I be in more than one place at one time. Review of those meetings led to realistic planning of how much time each engagement would take and, more important, what I actually needed to attend. In looking at the motivations that created overscheduling, I would be better able to balance work and personal demands. Eliminating the unnecessary would help to create a more feasible schedule that could be followed.

Attempting to alleviate some of the various multi-tasking elements of my schedule, I set goals for the month: enjoying the holiday season with a limited amount of stress, closing out a budget for the current year, creating a forecast and budget for the next year. Channeling energy on goals helped not only to prioritize the schedule, but also to quiet distracting thoughts. The sense of accomplishment also increased as each day something would be accomplished in support of the goals. This framework gave appropriate time to each task and in turn avoided calendar mishaps. The schedule would only fail if rushing when planning a meeting or a social engagement. When I took the time to actually check my book, mistakes were less likely to occur.

By week two, the holiday party season was derailing the productivity at work as well as my diet regime. Each year, the season seemed to creep in earlier and earlier. In the last two weeks of December, unlucky employees who pulled office duty would be spending the holiday alone as most people clear out by the twenty-second. Impromptu parties would spring up in offices along the corridor daily as gift baskets arrived from vendors. These deliveries, writing holiday cards, and chocolate eating were all distractions that persuaded my inner slacker to cave in. In high school and college, we described this condition as Senioritis, which is the undeniable urge to blow off all work to party at the campus pub. In adulthood the ennui of the year budgeting was being challenged by the notion of drinking champagne in the middle of the afternoon at the company luncheon.

The first few weeks were running like a well-oiled machine by adhering to the following schedule:

- Current projects planning—1 hour
- Budgeting—2 hours
- Returning calls—1 hour
- Lunch—1½ hours
- Meetings—2 hours
- Organization—15 minutes at the day's beginning and 15 at the day's end

In a way, it was like being in kindergarten again when play time, lunch time, and reading time would all be carefully slotted. The teacher always made everything fit in that short day. Thinking about the day in segments helped to stay focused.

Gaining control of the schedule was empowering, while taking it for granted resulted in trouble. I realized quickly that although my state of awareness had been changed, the state of those around me had not. Earlier in the month, a colleague would park himself in the guest chair, coffee in hand, and with no intention of leaving. I would say nothing. Spending time for an office visit may have been accommodated last month, but this month there was no time to spare. Instead of continuing with the e-mail, I dropped everything to give full attention, honoring *unitasking*, but not my schedule. So as not to be burned by this scenario twice, a new way to deal with the situation arose after several minutes, when the conversation took a natural pause. Dipping a toe into the cool social water, the colleague was informed of my master plan. With a smile, I explained that it was great to catch up, but I should get back to the binging e-mail and flashing voice mail. Nonplussed, the colleague smiled and said, "Cool, catch you later." The peace had begun that day and it had begun with me.

It was the best of times and the worst of times. Holiday shopping and multitasking teamed up once again as my dual nemesis. There is an old cliché that says, "If you want something done give it to a busy person." As the assigned busy shopper in the family, my duties included buying gifts for my siblings as well as for and from my parents. Getting a surprise gift was a distant memory as I purchased my own gifts, leaving me to wonder what the point of gift giving was at all. Despite retail guidance, the holiday season does not begin in late August when Treasure Island adorns its windows with an eight-foot faux spruce, it begins when my siblings call to ask what everyone in the family wants in their stocking this year.

I have suspicions that the same Lord & Taylor gift

card is making its way around the family for the past several holidays. I scoff at the "regift," where other family members embrace it, notably without stress. While perhaps impersonal, using the Internet and buying gift cards relieved much of my holiday angst, but I vowed next year that less shopping would equal more fun. This elf was officially retiring. Viva la gift card!

Even though misery is supposed to love company, living in the moment caused a new awareness of those around me who seemed to be rushing through life with hands full. A young mother goes for a run with a high-tech baby stroller. I saw a man walking down the street unbelievably flossing his teeth, illustrating that some can do more indeed than walk and chew gum at the same time. Even the local yoga studio was offering power yoga, whose paradoxical intent was to enjoy the practice of yoga while boosting your cardio. We thrive on getting things done faster, but not necessarily better. Studies have been noted on television and in magazines about multitasking not only making people less efficient, but also causing problems with short-term memory.

Overwhelmed with choices and stimuli, it is no surprise that tasks get lost in the shuffle. With our plates overstuffed and our in-boxes full, messages are often not gotten. Even cell phones have call waiting. No place is safe from the bombardment, even the treadmill at the gym. The monitor flashes MTV, causing a mental as well as a physical workout, taxing the mind and body. Cases of attention deficit disorder are on the rise. By definition, ADD includes several adjectives that could be used to describe me, inattentiveness, hyperactivity, and impulsivity. I was certain that I did not have the medical disorder, but was aware that technology was moving faster than my brain could manage. Observing my six-year-old nephew, I noted his ambidextrous Game Boy ability. It is a talent that I will never acquire. For Nicholas, the trait is innate.

As an antidote to the society where instant messaging and getting paged are the norm, more and more people are romanced by the daily respites. In an ironic way, the day spa's fifteen-minute massage is all there is time for as the busier-than-thou movement can only devote precious minutes to regain balance or, in the words of my best friend, "get human again." In my town alone, seven day spas have opened in the past year, indicating the need for daily escape. A magazine editor friend of mine finds so much stress in her career that she plans spa vacations to recharge her batteries at least every six months. She lives to get away to quiet places, outside the city, where she relishes time alone with her thoughts. Escaping from the rat race is the motivation for most vacations, making these trips more therapeutic than the routine trip to Epcot. They indicate a societal trend. Similar to the downshifting taking place in other countries, Americans are getting more involved in taking care of themselves. As a result, yoga studios and day spas are seeing a tremendous growth in business as people look for daily Zen.

As for my daily Zen, the high of completing a task from beginning to end was creating a healthier existence. Leaving work at the end of the day was usually hectic. A sense of panic would set in as I lamented over the jobs that did not get completed that day. Already an eye was being cast to the next day's double workload. At times, the "to do" list would keep me up at night. Now, just fifteen minutes of "office recon" a day, the expectation for the next day was set. This put me at peace when closing the door to the office.

A classic Zen story goes as follows: A Japanese warrior who is captured and thrown into prison is unable to sleep as he fears what will happen the next day. The Zen master comes to him, saying, "Tomorrow is not real. It is an illusion. The only reality is now." After hearing this guidance, the warrior becomes peaceful and falls asleep.

The most important thing I learned this month was to face the uncertainty head-on. Each day there would be some dreaded task, a phone call, a workout, or even an unpalatable errand. Tackling that first made way for a better day and most of the time the anxiety about the task was the problem, not the task itself. Taking time to look at where the time was spent helped me to recognize the necessary things. Once a clock watcher and daily planner extraordinaire, I have begun to gain more appreciation for the everyday.

What I had set out to do this month was to take more time with each task at hand and hopefully to avoid mistakes and stress in daily life. Doing too many things at one time was tapping brain power and preventing full enjoyment of the holidays, which was true. But the deeper meaning came when addressing the social and work calendar. It was obvious that I was doing too much in a short amount of time and not experiencing any of it. The need for focus and priority were all a part of *unitasking*. With all the distractions that can be encountered in everyday life, it is easy to get off track. What my friends noticed about this month's me was a person who actually listened during conversations. To give someone your full attention amid the distractions of modern society is unfortunately considered a gift, not a given. I was no longer going to take that basic for granted.

Subtle changes appeared after the month's end; slowly, challenges arrived like wolves at the door. Equipped with new ways to deal with the multifacets of the multitasking life, I would keep one simple idea in mind. Decades from now, when looking back at my life, I do not want to wish that I had done something else. I do not want to be remembered as a person who did not listen to others or a friend who was too preoccupied to be supportive. And most of all, I do not want to wish my life away like a marked-up Filofax page. Instead, I choose to be in the moment, to focus on others, to prioritize tasks, and to trust that in the end it will all work out.

With the goals for the month achieved, I raised a champagne glass, noting the passing of another year. Perhaps thoughts may have leaped to the new challenges laid out in next year's planner, but that would wait in due time. As for that moment, there was celebrating to do.